MW00768405

Drupal 6 Search Engine Optimization

Rank high in search engines with professional SEO tips, modules, and best practices for Drupal web sites

Ben Finklea

BIRMINGHAM - MUMBAI

Drupal 6 Search Engine Optimization

Copyright © 2009 Packt Publishing

All rights reserved. No part of this book may be reproduced, stored in a retrieval system, or transmitted in any form or by any means, without the prior written permission of the publisher, except in the case of brief quotations embedded in critical articles or reviews.

Every effort has been made in the preparation of this book to ensure the accuracy of the information presented. However, the information contained in this book is sold without warranty, either express or implied. Neither the author, nor Packt Publishing, and its dealers and distributors will be held liable for any damages caused or alleged to be caused directly or indirectly by this book.

Packt Publishing has endeavored to provide trademark information about all of the companies and products mentioned in this book by the appropriate use of capitals. However, Packt Publishing cannot guarantee the accuracy of this information.

First published: September 2009

Production Reference: 1040909

Published by Packt Publishing Ltd.
32 Lincoln Road
Olton
Birmingham, B27 6PA, UK.

ISBN 978-1-847198-22-8

www.packtpub.com

Cover Image by Harmeet Singh (singharmeet@yahoo.com)

Credits

Author
Ben Finklea

Reviewers
John K. Murphy

Michael Ruoss

Acquisition Editor
Douglas Paterson

Development Editor
Dilip Venkatesh

Technical Editor
Mehul Shetty

Indexer
Monica Ajmera

Editorial Team Leader
Akshara Aware

Project Team Leader
Priya Mukherji

Project Coordinator
Zainab Bagasrawala

Proofreader
Lynda Sliwoski

Production Coordinator
Dolly Dasilva

Cover Work
Dolly Dasilva

Drawing Coordinator
Nilesh Mohite

About the Author

Ben Finklea is the founder and CEO of Volacci, an online marketing company in Austin, Texas. It is the best job in the world.

He entered the world of online marketing in 1995, when he founded a web design company from his dormitory room at Texas A&M University. After graduation, he worked in various capacities in sales and marketing, from tiny start-ups to Apple. In 2001, he founded Sprysoft, an e-commerce store that successfully sold over $5 million in software (online) to students, teachers, and schools. He formed SpryDev Online Marketing in 2005, to use the techniques and processes learned at Sprysoft, to help other businesses sell online. SpryDev grew quickly and changed names to Volacci in 2008.

He and the Volacci team provide Search Engine Optimization, Paid Search, and Conversions Consulting to a varied client base, ranging from local real estate agents to Fortune 500 companies. Their goal is to be the best Drupal SEO company on the planet.

You can hear him on the Volacci SEO podcasts and videos, and read his blog at `www.Volacci.com`. His Twitter name is BenFinklea.

He spends his free time reading, writing, volunteering at his church, and raising two sons with his wife of 14 years. He used to do cool things like collecting comic books and baseball cards, paintball, and playing video games. He's looking forward to doing all those things again when his kids get a little older.

He lives near Austin, Texas.

Acknowledgement

I would like to thank the Drupal community for making Drupal the best development platform on the planet for SEO. I stood on the shoulders of giants.

Specifically, I would like to thank the following:

Dries Buytaert: Drupal's founder, fearless guide, and voice in the wilderness.

Jeff Robbins and the rest of the Lullabot crew for the Lullabot Podcast & videos.

Angie Byron for your awesome tutorials and for being there, unasked, when I needed help

Bryan House and Robert Douglas, at Acquia, for your guidance.

And to the following SEO-related Drupal module creators, maintainers, and contributors—This book just isn't possible without your commitment to Drupal. In no particular order:

Kris Vanderwater and Jakub Suchy, who helped me write the new and improved Drupal SEO Checklist module.

Mike Carter: Google Analytics module.

Alexander Hass: Google Analytics module.

Zohar Stolar: Top Searches module.

Nicolas Thompson: Page Title and Global Redirect modules.

John Albin: Page Title module.

Jeff Eaton: Token module.

Greg Knaddison: Token and PathAuto modules.

Mike Ryan: Token and PathAuto modules.

Frederik 'Freso' S. Olesen: PathAuto module.

Dave Reid: Path Redirect, XML Sitemap 2.x, Google News sitemap, and Mollom modules (and for that time you helped me get to my plane on time at the Denver airport).

Robrecht Jacques: Meta tags module.

Alberto Paderno: Meta tags module.

Matthew Loar: XML Sitemap module.

Kiam LaLuno: XML Sitemap module.

Moshe Weitzman: Syndication module (and many more).

Eric Schaefer: Scheduler module.

Arto Bendiken: RDF module.

Frank Febbraro: Open Calais module.

Edward Z. Yang: HTML Purifier module.

Nick Schoonens: Google Optimizer module.

Adam Boyse: Google News sitemap module.

David K Norman: URL list module.

Nic Ivy: Site map module.

Fredrik Jonsson: Site map module, and

The unnamed module developer — you know who you are.

I would also like to thank the following:

My family: Beverly — my beautiful wife — who sacrificed so much of herself so I could create this book. In the time I wrote this book, she worked a full-time teaching job in the Genetics department at UT Austin, moved our family into a new home, prepared our old house for sale, sold it, got the kids into new schools, set up our church with a new financial system, prepared meals for people in need, loved on our kids while I was gone, and changed far more than her fair share of dirty diapers. Moreover, she helped, encouraged, and loved me which is more than all of the rest of it combined. Writing this book fulfills a lifelong dream but you are still the best thing that ever happened to me.

My sons, Andrew and John, who always welcome me home with such enthusiasm and affection.

Erik Wagner, Andrew Cao, Josh Ward, Luke Stenis, and the rest of the Volacci team whose dedication to our clients is second to none. Kudos!

Matt Cutts, John Mueller, and others at Google, who have helped me all along the way. You have been surprisingly approachable, and I am deeply grateful.

Jimmy Eierdam, my trainer at the N. Austin YMCA, who helped me work off the stress, and encouraged me to keep going when I got discouraged.

The friendly staff at the Greenlawn Crossing Starbucks in Round Rock, Texas, who provided the jet fuel and comfy chairs that were so essential to my writing process.

Last, but not the least, the talent at Packt who gave me this opportunity. The next round of beers is on me. I think that's actually in my contract!

About the Reviewers

John K. Murphy is a graduate of the University of West Virginia, and has been wrapped up in computers and software development since the 1980s. When he is not buried in a book or jumping out of an airplane, he works as an IT consultant.

He lives with his wife and two children in Pittsburgh, PA, and is currently obsessing about the Internet of Things.

Michael Ruoss is a consultant at Optaros. His main technical skills lie in the development of PHP/MySQL frameworks. He holds a Master's Degree in Computer Science from Swiss Federal Institute of Technology in Zurich. Within the engagement at Optaros, he gained much experience in the integration of Drupal, Magento, Alfresco, and other CMS and e-commerce solutions.

Table of Contents

Preface

"There can be only one!" —The Highlander

"If you are not first in Google then your competition certainly is."
—Ben Finklea

At its heart, Drupal is a way for people to build great web sites in a short period of time. It's packaged up with some compelling features like user logins, RSS, version control, an advanced theme layer, and solid core code. There are bundled releases (Acquia Drupal and Open Atrium) that take Drupal further, faster. There are great theme web sites (`www.topnotchthemes.com`) that make your site look just like you want it to. There are terrific training videos (`www.lullabot.com`), and hundreds of forums where you can find answers to any question you might have. But, Drupal is not perfect.

Despite its advantages, many Drupal web sites suffer with poor search engine rankings. The thing that makes Drupal so powerful—its flexibility—also means that it takes some work to get it configured just the right way for the search engines.

That's where Drupal 6 Search Engine Optimization comes in.

With this book and basic Drupal 6 knowledge, that is, how to log in, create content, and install modules—you can build a perfectly optimized web site. Each chapter uses easy, step-by-step instructions to walk you through the Drupal Search Engine Optimization (SEO) modules, configurations, and content you will need. Advanced topics include things like site organization, A/B testing, and automatic content tagging to maximize SEO. If you want a significant advantage over competitors who are not using Drupal, and to maximize the return on investment of your Drupal 6 web site, then this is the book for you.

What this book covers

Chapter 1, The Tools That You'll Need, covers all the tools you're going to need for Drupal SEO. From Drupal and all the great modules available for SEO to setting up a Google account, this chapter is foundational to the rest of this book.

Chapter 2, Keyword Research, explains all the tools you're going to need to do keyword research, from Drupal stats in your own web site to all the great tools available online. Keyword research is one of the most important things you'll do in SEO, so make sure you've taken the time to do it right.

Chapter 3, On-Page Optimization, explores the most important aspects of on-page SEO for your Drupal site, which are Page Titles and Paths.

Chapter 4, More On-Page Optimization, covers more of the all-important aspects of on-page SEO for your Drupal site.

Chapter 5, Sitemaps, discusses the origin of sitemaps and how they're used to make sure your entire site is crawled by the search engines. It also teaches you how to make a user-friendly sitemap for your site visitors.

Chapter 6, robots.txt, .htaccess, and W3C Validation, teaches you some of the most technical aspects of a good SEO.

Chapter 7, RSS Feeds, Site Speed, and SEO Testing, helps you get your web site Search Engine Optimized. It teaches you about RSS Feeds, PageRank, Drupal's built-in caching, and checking your site with SEOmoz.

Chapter 8, Content is King, teaches you how to get good content and search engine optimize it. It also teaches you how to maintain the content and keep it search engine-optimized.

Chapter 9, Taking Control of Your Content, teaches how to maintain your content and gain control over it. It also teaches how to keep your content compliant and free from spam with the use of various modules.

Chapter 10, Increasing the Conversion Rate of Your Drupal Web site, explores the three main types of web sites and their conversion goals. It also covers the Usability and A/B testing techniques.

Appendix A explains how to avoid ten common SEO mistakes.

Appendix B provides you with the Drupal SEO Checklist.

Appendix C covers the Drupal SEO case study for the Acquia product launch.

What you need for this book

A basic understanding of Drupal will be helpful—what a node is, how to create nodes, how to log in to the admin sections of your Drupal site, and how to properly install and enable a module. No knowledge of SEO will be assumed, but a basic knowledge of search engines is expected.

Who this book is for

Maybe you're a web site owner who wants to get more leads and sales from his web site. Maybe you're a Drupal web developer and your customers are asking you how to increase the return on investment of their web site. Or perhaps you're a non-profit, that is looking for more donations and volunteers. Maybe you're someone else entirely, there are almost as many good reasons to rank well in Google as there are web sites.

No matter your reason, you hold in your hands the knowledge that you need to rank at the top of the search engines, and turn visitors into paying customers for your business. Each page of this book tells you exactly what you'll need to do, to properly search engine optimize your web site. If you're relatively new to Drupal, just follow the easy, step-by-step instructions and screenshots. If you're an old hand, skip past the basic steps and review the best configuration options for each module. I've boiled down years of experience in Drupal, online marketing, monetization, dozens of modules, some tips, and a few tricks into a powerful potion of Drupal SEO goodness.

Conventions

In this book, you will find a number of styles of text that distinguish between different kinds of information. Here are some examples of these styles, and an explanation of their meaning.

Code words in text are shown as follows: "Let's take a deeper look at each directive used in the Drupal `robots.txt` file".

New terms and **important words** are shown in bold. Words that you see on the screen, in menus or dialog boxes for example, appear in our text like this: " I added the site logo file into the **Test URLs** box".

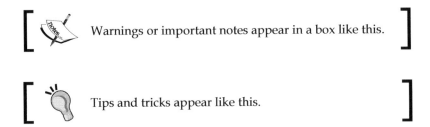

Warnings or important notes appear in a box like this.

Tips and tricks appear like this.

Reader feedback

Feedback from our readers is always welcome. Let us know what you think about this book—what you liked or may have disliked. Reader feedback is important for us to develop titles that you really get the most out of.

To send us general feedback, simply drop an email to feedback@packtpub.com, and mention the book title in the subject of your message.

If there is a book that you need and would like to see us publish, please send us a note in the **SUGGEST A TITLE** form on www.packtpub.com or email suggest@packtpub.com.

If there is a topic that you have expertise in and you are interested in either writing or contributing to a book, see our author guide on www.packtpub.com/authors.

Customer support

Now that you are the proud owner of a Packt book, we have a number of things to help you to get the most from your purchase.

Errata

Although we have taken every care to ensure the accuracy of our content, mistakes do happen. If you find a mistake in one of our books—maybe a mistake in the text or code—we would be grateful if you would report this to us. By doing so, you can save other readers from frustration, and help us to improve subsequent versions of this book. If you find any errata, please report them by visiting http://www.packtpub.com/support, selecting your book, clicking on the **let us know** link, and entering the details of your errata. Once your errata are verified, your submission will be accepted and the errata added to any list of existing errata. Any existing errata can be viewed by selecting your title from http://www.packtpub.com/support.

Piracy

Piracy of copyrighted material on the Internet is an ongoing problem across all media. At Packt, we take the protection of our copyright and licenses very seriously. If you come across any illegal copies of our works in any form on the Internet, please provide us with the location address or web site name immediately so that we can pursue a remedy.

Please contact us at copyright@packtpub.com with a link to the suspected pirated material.

We appreciate your help in protecting our authors, and our ability to bring you valuable content.

Questions

You can contact us at questions@packtpub.com if you are having a problem with any aspect of the book, and we will do our best to address it.

1
The Tools You'll Need

Congratulations! You're about to embark on a fun and interesting journey into the world of online marketing. Whether you're trying to sell more products, generate leads, or get more pageviews on your sponsors ads, **Search Engine Optimization (SEO)** will take you where you want to go.

And, you're using Drupal 6! You've picked a great platform for building your web site. It's widely held that Drupal is one of the best choices if you want to rank well in the search engines. I personally believe that it's hands-down the best possible platform for SEO. I've seen clients triple their traffic within a few weeks of switching from a lesser platform. Believe it—Drupal is the best! But, you already knew that, didn't you? In this chapter, we're going to dive right in and cover some of the top tips for Drupal SEO:

- Drupal—which version you should use
- How to install 99% of modules
- The essential SEO modules that you'll need for your Drupal site
- Installing and using the SEO Checklist module
- Setting up a Google account
- Installing Google analytics and Webmaster Tools on your site
- Some great paid tools to help you with your SEO

Helpful web sites:

There are some great resources online to help you along:

`www.DrupalSEObook.com`: The web site of this book. Visit for additional tips, updates, module suggestions, and to discuss Drupal SEO. The author often participates here so it's a great place to ask questions.

`groups.drupal.org/search-engine-optimization`: The Drupal SEO group on `www.Drupal.org`.

`tips.webdesign10.com/drupal-seo`: Another resource for Drupal SEO tips.

The right tools make the project go smoothly. When you decide to SEO your Drupal 6 web site, you'll need the following:

Drupal 6

You can download Drupal 6 from two sources:

- `Drupal.org`: This is where you can get the latest release of the open-source Drupal 6.

- `Acquia.com`: Acquia is a company co-founded by Dries Buytart (the founder of Drupal) and Jay Batson. Acquia has produced a corporate version of Drupal, creatively called Acquia Drupal. Acquia Drupal has some of the better modules pre-installed and provides some great extra services like uptime monitoring, version updates, and advanced support to your installation and modules. Downloading and installing it is free but the services do cost a bit extra—starting at a few hundred dollars per year. That's well worth the extras you get.

Are you running a corporate site and you're not quite up to speed on Drupal? Consider signing up for Acquia's support services. Acquia Network subscriptions provide commercial-grade support and network services for all Drupal 6.x web sites (not just Acquia Drupal) to help you implement Drupal with confidence. Visit `http://acquia.com/` for more information.

Modules

A module is a community-created plugin that enhances Drupal's core functionality. From XML sitemaps to better page titles, modules are crucial to the search engine optimization of any Drupal site. Installing modules is easy and once you know how to install one, you probably know how to install them all.

 For a complete explanation of installing modules, check out the following links: http://drupal.org/node/120641 and http://drupal.org/node/120642.

Installing 99% of Drupal modules:

In the upcoming chapters, you'll come across a lot of Drupal modules. You need to carry out the following steps in order install 99% of Drupal modules:

1. Download the module from http://drupal.org/project/Modules and extract it.

2. FTP to your Drupal site. Drop the extracted module folder into the sites/all/modules folder (if that directory is not there then create it).

3. Using your browser, visit http://www.yourDrupalsite.com/user and log in.

4. Now visit http://www.yourDrupalsite.com/admin/build/modules/. If you forget this URL, just go to the admin page and click the **Modules** link.

5. Select the checkbox next to the module that you just installed. If needed, also tic any sub-modules that you just installed.

6. Click on the **Save Configuration** button. In a couple of seconds, the newly selected module will install itself. Any errors will appear in red.

7. Go to http://www.yourDrupalsite.com/admin/user/permissions and set the permissions for that module so that different **roles** can use or administer the new functionality that the module has added (not required for all modules).

8. Go to http://www.yourDrupalsite.com/admin and you'll see links to customize the settings of your newly installed module.

Installing the remaining 1% Drupal modules

If the module isn't working, be sure to read the README.txt file that came with the module. Sometimes, there are extra steps required to fully install a module.

Drush: The alternative to manual Drupal module installation

If you're comfortable with using the Unix command line, you should consider **Drush**. Drush is a module created by Moshe Weitzman that provides a command line shell and Unix scripting interface for Drupal. After you install it, you'll be able to use commands like drush dl modulename and drush enable modulename to install and enable modules. No trips to drupal.org and no admin screens so it's very fast.

Essential SEO modules

Now that you know how to install modules, there are several that you'll need in order to optimize your Drupal site.

What follows is a list of the non-core Drupal modules you'll use most often for SEO. (Non-core means not included in the base Drupal installation. However, something might be included in Acquia Drupal so check your Modules admin screen first!) We'll cover almost all of these in more detail later in the book. You can either download them all and install them on your site or grab them one at a time as you work on each SEO task. Either way, don't enable them until you're clear what they do and how to configure them. Sometimes, careful setup is required to get the optimal benefit from a module.

- **SEO Checklist**: It provides a checklist with download links and admin shortcuts to most modules and tasks needed during the SEO process.
    - To download this module, follow this link: http://drupal.org/project/seo_checklist
    - To configure this module's settings, follow this link: http://www.yourDrupalsite.com/admin/settings/seochecklist
    - Step-by-step configuration instructions have been provided in this chapter

The SEO Checklist will help you save time

The Drupal SEO Checklist module helps you keep track of the SEO tasks needed for your site. It doesn't do any SEO by itself—it's a checklist that follows along nicely with this book. Links to download and configure most of the modules listed here are built into the SEO Checklist module. It also puts a date stamp on each task as you complete it so it's very handy if you're working on more than one site or you would like to report the work you've done to a boss or client.

- **Google Analytics**: It helps you keep track of visitors.
    - To download this module, follow this link:
      `http://drupal.org/project/google_analytics`
    - To configure this module's settings, follow this link:
      `http://www.yourDrupalsite.com/admin/settings/googleanalytics`
    - Step-by-step configuration instructions have been provided in this chapter

- **Page title**: It allows you to set `<title>` tags for nodes throughout your site.
    - To download this module, follow this link:
      `http://drupal.org/project/page_title`
    - Note: The Page title requires the Token module to function
      Download: `http://drupal.org/project/token`
    - To configure this module's settings, follow this link: `http://www.yourDrupalsite.com/admin/settings/page_title`
    - Step-by-step configuration instructions have been provided in Chapter 3, *On-Page Optimization*

- **Pathauto**: It automatically creates search engine friendly URLs based on the title of your content.
    - To download this module, follow this link:
      `http://drupal.org/project/pathauto`
    - To configure this module's settings, follow this link: `http://www.yourDrupalsite.com/admin/settings/pathauto`
    - Step-by-step configuration instructions have been provided in Chapter 3, *On-Page Optimization*

- **Path redirect**: It helps create proper redirects.
  - ○ To download this module, follow this link:
    `http://drupal.org/project/path_redirect`
  - ○ To configure this module's settings, follow this link:
    `http://www.yourDrupalsite.com/admin/settings/`
    `path-redirect`
  - ○ Visit the following link in order to create and change paths:
    `http://www.yourDrupalsite.com/admin/settings/`
    `build/path-redirect`
  - ○ Step-by-step configuration instructions have been provided in Chapter 3, *On-Page Optimization*

- **Global redirect**: It fixes some common URL problems when clean URLs and Pathauto are turned on.
  - ○ To download this module, follow this link:
    `http://drupal.org/project/globalredirect`
  - ○ To configure this module's settings, follow this link:
    `http://www.yourDrupalsite.com/admin/settings/`
    `globalredirect`
  - ○ Step-by-step configuration instructions have been provided in Chapter 3, *On-Page Optimization*

- **Taxonomy title**: It allows you to set `<title>` tags for taxonomy terms throughout your site.
  - ○ To download this module, follow this link:
    `http://drupal.org/project/taxonomy_title`
  - ○ There are no links to the admin site. Set taxonomy `<title>` on each term page.

- **Meta tags** (formerly known as the Nodewords module): It gives you full control of the meta tags on your site, nodes, categories, views, and so on.
  - ○ To download this module, follow this link:
    `http://drupal.org/project/nodewords`
  - ○ To configure this module's settings, follow this link: `http://`
    `www.yourDrupalsite.com/admin/user/permissions`
  - ○ Step-by-step configuration instructions have been provided in Chapter 4, *More On-Page Optimization*

- **XML Site map**: It creates a **Sitemaps.org** compliant, search engine readable, dynamic sitemap.
    - ○ To download this module, follow this link: `http://drupal.org/project/xmlsitemap`
    - ○ Note: Be sure to get the 2.0 or higher version of the module
    - ○ Step-by-step configuration instructions have been provided in Chapter 5, *Sitemaps*

- **URL list**: It creates a plain text sitemap that lists every URL on your Drupal site.
    - ○ Use it if you can't use the XML Sitemap module
    - ○ To download this module, follow this link: `http://drupal.org/project/urllist`
    - ○ To configure this module's settings, follow this link: `http://www.yourDrupalsite.com/admin/settings/urllist`
    - ○ Step-by-step configuration instructions have been provided in Chapter 5, *Sitemaps*

- **Site map**: It creates a plain text sitemap.
    - ○ To download this module, follow this link: `http://drupal.org/project/site_map`
    - ○ To configure this module's settings, follow this link: `http://www.yourDrupalsite.com/admin/settings/sitemap`
    - ○ Step-by-step configuration instructions have been provided in Chapter 5, *Sitemaps*

- **Syndication**: It offers a web page which centralizes all of the RSS feeds generated by Drupal.
    - ○ To download this module, follow this link: `http://drupal.org/project/syndication`
    - ○ To configure this module's settings, follow this link: `http://www.yourDrupalsite.com/admin/content/syndication`
    - ○ Step-by-step configuration instructions have been provided in Chapter 6, *RSS Feeds, Site Speed, and SEO Testing*

- **Menu attributes**: It allows you to specify some additional attributes for menu items such as id, name, class, style, and rel.
    - To download this module, follow this link:
      `http://drupal.org/project/menu_attributes`
    - To configure this module's settings, follow this link:
      `http://www.yourDrupalsite.com/admin/content/menu_attributes`

- **Site verification**: It assists with search engine site ownership verification.
    - To download this module, follow this link:
      `http://drupal.org/project/site_verify`
    - To configure this module's settings, follow this link: `http://www.yourDrupalsite.com/admin/build/site-verify`
    - Step-by-step configuration instructions have been provided in this chapter

- **Scheduler**: It allows you to schedule when nodes are published.
    - To download this module, follow this link:
      `http://drupal.org/project/scheduler`
    - To configure this module's settings, follow this link: `http://www.yourDrupalsite.com/admin/settings/scheduler`
    - Step-by-step configuration instructions have been provided in Chapter 8, *Content is King*

- **Read more link**: It allows you to create customized, SEO-friendly **Read more** links.
    - To download this module, follow this link:
      `http://drupal.org/project/ed_readmore`
    - To configure this module's settings, follow this link: `http://www.yourDrupalsite.comadmin/settings/ed_readmore`

- **HTML Purifier**: It helps fix poor html on user generated content.
    - To download this module, follow this link:
      `http://drupal.org/project/htmlpurifier`
    - To configure this module's settings, follow this link:
      `http://www.yourDrupalsite.com/admin/settings/filters`

○   Step-by-step configuration instructions have been provided in Chapter 9, *Taking Control of Your Content*

- **Mollom**: It provides spam protection via the powerful Mollom service.

    ○   To download this module, follow this link: `http://drupal.org/project/mollom`

    ○   To configure this module's settings, follow this link: `http://www.yourDrupalsite.com/admin/settings/mollom`

    ○   Step-by-step configuration instructions have been provided in Chapter 9, *Taking Control of Your Content*

Optional SEO modules

There are a few more SEO modules which are optional. Let's have a look at them.

- **RobotsTxt**: It dynamically generates the `robots.txt` file on multiple Drupal installations.

    ○   Make use of this module if you have multiple sites running off a single Drupal installation and you need different `robots.txt` files for each site

    ○   To download this module, follow this link: `http://drupal.org/project/robotstxt`

- **Google News sitemap generator**: It creates an XML sitemap that meets the specification for Google News.

    ○   Use if you're running a news or media web site.

    ○   To download this module, follow this link: `http://drupal.org/project/googlenews`

    ○   To configure this module's settings, follow this link: `http://www.yourDrupalsite.com/admin/settings/googlenews`

    ○   Step-by-step configuration instructions have been provided in Chapter 5, *Sitemaps*

- **Top Searches**: It shows you what people are searching for on your site.

    ○   Use if you want to create more interesting content for your site and you want to know what people are looking for

    ○   To download this module, follow this link: `http://drupal.org/project/top_searches`

○ To configure this module's settings, follow this link:
`http://www.yourDrupalsite.com/admin/settings/`
`top_searches`

○ Step-by-step configuration instructions have been provided in Chapter 2, *Keyword Research*

- **Open Calais**: It provides access to the free OpenCalais tool from Reuters.

    ○ Use if you want automatic tagging of your content based on people, companies, organizations, books, albums, places, facts, etc. Typically used for news sites or companies that interact often with the media although others may benefit as well.

    ○ To download this module, follow this link:
    `http://drupal.org/project/opencalais`

    ○ To configure this module's settings, follow this link: `http://`
    `www.yourDrupalsite.com/admin/settings/calais`

    ○ Step-by-step configuration instructions have been provided in Chapter 9, *Taking Control of Your Content*

- **RDF**: It provides RDF functionality and interoperability.

    ○ Required for the Open Calais module.

    ○ To download this module, follow this link:
    `http://drupal.org/project/rdf`

    ○ To configure this module's settings, follow this link: `http://`
    `www.yourDrupalsite.com/admin/settings/rdf`

    ○ Step-by-step configuration instructions have been provided in Chapter 9, *Taking Control of Your Content*

- **More Like This**: It provides links to related content based on taxonomies or words you specify.

    ○ Works very well with the OpenCalais module

    ○ To download this module, follow this link:
    `http://drupal.org/project/morelikethis`

    ○ To configure this module's settings, follow this link:
    `http://www.yourDrupalsite.com/admin/settings/`
    `morelikethis`

    ○ Step-by-step configuration instructions have been provided in Chapter 9, *Taking Control of Your Content*

- **Autoload**: It does not provide functionality directly. It is required by the More Like This module.
  - ○ To download this module, follow this link:
    `http://drupal.org/project/autoload`
  - ○ Step-by-step configuration instructions have been provided in Chapter 9, *Taking Control of Your Content*

- **Google Website Optimizer**: It integrates your site with Google's A/B and multivariate tool.
  - ○ Use if you want to do A/B testing on your Drupal site
  - ○ To download this module, follow this link:
    `http://drupal.org/project/google_website_optimizer`
  - ○ To configure this module's settings, follow this link: `http://www.yourDrupalsite.com/admin/settings/google_website_optimizer`
  - ○ Step-by-step configuration instructions have been provided in Chapter 10, *Increasing the Conversion Rate of Your Drupal Web site*

- **Node Hierarchy**: It helps create hierarchy in your site which is good for SEO.
  - ○ To download this module, follow this link:
    `http://drupal.org/project/nodehierarchy`

- **Alinks**: It dynamically turns specific words on your site into links.
  - ○ To download this module, follow this link:
    `http://drupal.org/project/alinks`

- **Digg This**: It facilitates links to the popular social bookmarking site Digg.
  - ○ To download this module, follow this link:
    `http://drupal.org/project/diggthis`

- **Service Links**: It adds links to several popular social bookmarking sites.
  - ○ To download this module, follow this link:
    `http://drupal.org/project/service_links`

Non-SEO modules

There are so many good, helpful modules; it's hard to mention them all. Here are a few non-SEO modules that I consider to be a must for any site I'm working on.

- **Administration Menu**: It makes it quick and easy to get to all the admin functions of your web site.
  - ○ To download this module, follow this link:
    `http://drupal.org/project/admin_menu`
- **Backup and Migrate**: It simplifies the task of backing up and restoring your Drupal database or migrating data from one Drupal site to another.
  - ○ To download this module, follow this link:
    `http://drupal.org/project/backup_migrate`
- **Devel**: It makes it easy to generate a bunch of nodes, taxonomies, and users for testing purposes. It has other helpful functions as well.
  - ○ To download this module, follow this link:
    `http://drupal.org/project/devel`
- **Notify**: It sends periodic emails with details of all changes to a site.
  - ○ Use if you want to review all posts, forums, or comments posted to your site. Great for responding to comments as they happen.
  - ○ To download this module, follow this link:
    `http://drupal.org/project/notify`
- **Search 404**: Instead of a file not found error if a page is missing, it does a search on the keywords in the URL to show possible matches.
  - ○ To download this module, follow this link:
    `http://drupal.org/project/search404`

PHP memory limits and module installation

If you install a lot of modules in Drupal then you may come across the dreaded "White Screen of Death". It often occurs when you visit the **Administer | Modules** page; you'll see nothing but a white screen. This means that PHP—the language that Drupal is written in – has run out of memory. There are several ways to increase the allotted memory. The easiest is to add the line `php_value memory_limit 32M` to your `.htaccess` file in the Drupal root. You can adjust this to 48M, 64M or even higher, but 32M typically works fine and conserves memory. Don't just max it out as that's the amount of memory that Drupal will use for each visitor and it adds up quickly, especially on shared servers. There are other options if this doesn't work. To find out more, visit `http://drupal.org/node/31819`.

Drupal SEO Checklist module

The **Drupal SEO Checklist** module is the first one that I install when I begin working on a site. Carry out the following steps to download and install the Drupal SEO Checklist module:

1. Download the SEO Checklist module from the following link, `http://drupal.org/project/seo_checklist` and install it just like a normal Drupal module. Refer to the earlier part of this chapter for step-by-step module installation instructions.

2. Visit the following link, `http://www.yourDrupalsite.com/admin/settings/seochecklist` or go to your admin screen and click on **Administer | Site configuration | SEO Checklist** link. Then, you'll be able to see the SEO Checklist admin page screen, as shown in the following screenshot:

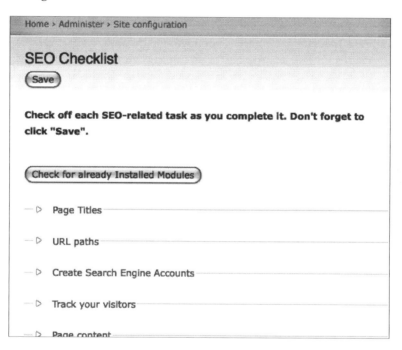

3. Find out which modules you already have installed by clicking on the **Check for already Installed Modules** button. It will check off any modules you've already installed.

4. Go through each section of the SEO Checklist admin page installing each module or completing each task. Be sure to check off each item as you go and click the **Save** button.

While it's not necessary to install this module, it will save you hours of research and hunting down the modules you need for proper SEO.

Google Account

Google is the undisputed leader in search. One way that they stay on top is by providing tools to help web site owners manage their sites. Among other things, they've created Google Analytics, Google Webmaster Tools, and Google Site Optimizer—all three essential to a good SEO campaign. Oh! And they're free. To access all this SEO goodness, you'll need to set up a Google Account.

Create an account for each company

If you're doing SEO for more than one company, keep them all separate. Set up a Google Account for yourself plus one for each client. If a client has more than one web site, put them all under that client's account. With many of Google's services, like Analytics, you can assign yourself as administrator of each account so you can access everything with one login. Thanks, Google!

Setting up a Google Account

Carry out the following steps to set up a Google account:

1. Go to `https://www.google.com/accounts/NewAccount`.

2. Fill out your information. Be sure to use a valid email address.

3. Read the Terms of Service and then click the **I accept. Create my account.** button.

4. You'll see a screen that says, **In order to verify that the email address associated with your account is correct, we have sent an email message to yourname@yourDrupalsite.com. To activate your Google account, please access your email and click on the link provided.**

5. You will receive an email with the subject **Google Email Verification** and with a link in the body to verify your account. Click on the link.

6. You should see the message, **Email Address Verified**.

Be sure to save your login in a safe place. You'll need it each time you access one of Google's services.

Analytics

In bygone years, people tracked visitors on their web site using server logs. While this is still accepted practice, it's difficult and time consuming to access enormous log files to figure out what's going on with your site. Several years ago, companies started releasing tools to make that process easier. They called their products **Analytics**.

Analytics packages help you track visitors on your web site — where they came from, what they do while on your site, where they are in the world, and if they bought your products or filled out your forms. It works by installing a small piece of JavaScript code in the footer of your site that pings a server every time a visitor loads a page. You could do this yourself but you'd have to process, filter, and store all that data on your own. A good analytics program is easier, faster, more robust, and in many cases free.

A good analytics program will help you learn which online marketing initiatives are cost effective and see how visitors interact with your site. With that information, you can make informed design improvements, drive targeted traffic, and increase your conversions and profits. Analytics won't make the tough decisions for you — they will give you the data you need to make those decisions.

A few common question that analytics can help answer are as follows:

How many unique visitors did I get over the last month?

What is my conversion rate?

How can I improve the visitor experience on my web site?

Why isn't anyone buying my product?

Are the negative comments on my blog affecting my sales?

How many sales came from Adwords vs. my SEO campaign?

Are visitors engaged by my front page or turned off?

It's important to install analytics as soon as possible, so that you can start to accumulate data about your site visitors. The more data you have, the better the reports and decisions you will be able to make. Depending on your site traffic, it may take weeks or months before you have enough meaningful data to put to use improving your site.

While you only need one analytics program, two will allow you to compare results and be sure that your stats are relatively in sync with each other. Different programs track data in different ways. If they're inconsistent then it could reveal a problem that needs to be fixed on your site.

Google Analytics

There are dozens of analytics packages out there and it's hard to beat Google's free suite which is simply called Google Analytics. It's easy to install, quick to get started, and has easy-to-read charts. Yet, it boasts very powerful features like advanced segmentation, customizable reporting, and industry benchmarking.

When using Google Analytics with Drupal, it's even better. It's easy to install, configure and test thanks to the Google Analytics module. The Google Analytics module was first created by Mike Carter and is now maintained by Alexander Hass. Thank you, gentlemen!

Creating a Google Analytics account and installing it on your Drupal site

To create a Google Analytics account and install it on your Drupal site, carry out the following steps:

1. Visit `http://www.google.com/analytics` and click the **Sign Up Now** link.

2. Log in using your Google account.

3. Fill out your web site information.

Web site URL:	Put the full URL of your site. If you use the www, then include it.
Account Name:	Google automatically enters the URL but that is often not the right choice. If you will ever have more than one web site that you track with Google Analytics then use an account name that is a bit more descriptive, such as your organization's name or even your name.
Time Zone Country:	Enter the country that your web site serves. For example, if your company serves Texas but you host your site in the UK, put **United States** as the country.
Time Zone:	Time zone will influence the dates and times that the analytics will report the traffic data from your site. You'll probably select the time zone that you work or live in.

4. Click on **Continue** and fill in your contact information.

5. Click on **Continue**. Here you'll read and agree to the **User Agreement**. You'll also notice that you're opted in to anonymously share your Google Analytics data. According to Google, **Shared data will be used to improve the services we provide you and will help create more powerful features for you to choose from**. There are two levels of sharing.

With other Google products only	It will only share your data with Google. This is more private and still gives you access to the enhanced features that may come out in the future.
Anonymously with Google and others	It will share your data more widely. Any identifying information about your site is removed and then it's mixed in with thousands of other sites' data. If you opt in at this level then you'll be able to benchmark your site with other sites in your industry. This can be helpful to see how you're doing compared to your competition.

6. Finally, click on **Create New Account**. You're done!

7. Now install the Google Analytics module. It installs normally like any other Drupal module. See earlier in this chapter for step-by-step module installation instructions. Here's the short version: Download the module, drop it into your `/sites/all/modules` folder, go to `/admin/build/modules`, and turn it on.

8. To configure the module, point your browser to `www.yourDrupalsite.com/admin/settings/googleanalytics` at the top of the page and you will be able see a screen similar to the following screenshot:

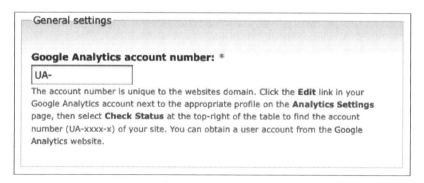

9. Go back to your Google Analytics account and you should see a number next to your URL name that starts with **UA-**, as shown in the following screenshot:

10. Copy and paste your site's UA number into your Drupal site. (Don't use mine! Get your own!) If you don't see this, click the **Analytics Settings** link, located at the upper left corner.

11. Under **User Specific Tracking Settings**, make sure that **Users cannot control whether they are tracked or not** option is selected. This makes sure that you're tracking all your visitors and they can't turn off the tracking.

12. Under **Role specific tracking settings**, you will have a few options. For most sites, you want to check everything except the **authenticated user** option, as shown in the following screenshot:

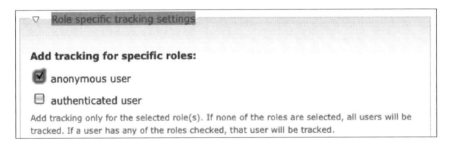

Role specific tracking settings is one of the best things about the Google Analytics module. One of the common problems with Google Analytics is that it tracks everything that happens on your site—even your own activity. So, if you visit your site a lot (which you probably should) then you'll skew your Analytics. Telling Drupal to not track admin users will dynamically show or not show Google's tracking code depending on if a user is the site admin. There are many uses for this. Say you don't want to track any of your company's users. Just give them a custom account type (like staff) and deselect the checkbox in the Google Analytics module. Clean, easy, and works like a champ!

13. Except for advanced needs, the rest of the settings should be left as the defaults. Click on **Save configuration**. You're done!

Common mistake when configuring the Google Analytics module

Under **Advanced settings**, there is a field called **Custom JavaScript Code**. DO NOT put your Google code there. If you've put your Google account information at the top of the admin page then the module will write all the code automatically. The **Custom JavaScript Code** field is for special code snippets that are added to the tracking code (refer to `drupal.org/node/248699`). If you put the full code there then you will track every user on your site twice. Not good!

Google's help pages say 'Once you've correctly installed your tracking code, you should allow up to 24 hours for data to appear in your account'. Check back tomorrow and you should see some data. It starts to get really interesting when you've accumulated several months worth of data. Be patient—it's well worth the wait.

Yahoo! Analytics

Yahoo! recently launched their own analytics package called Yahoo! Analytics. It's getting good reviews as an alternative to Google Analytics. As of this writing it's only available to Yahoo!'s search and display advertisers. For more information visit the following link: `http://web.analytics.yahoo.com/`.

Google Webmaster Tools

If you've got a site that shows up in Google then you need a **Google Webmaster Tools** account. The Google Webmaster Tools provide you with detailed reports about your pages' visibility on Google. It's one of the most direct ways that you can communicate with Google about your site. It allows you to upload an XML sitemap, see if there are any problems with your site and fix them. It even lets you control the Google spider so that it doesn't drag your site down with constant visits.

To use the tool, you need to verify your site. Fortunately, there is a great module called the **Site verification** module that helps you verify your site with the search engines. It was created and is maintained by Dave Reid. Thanks, Dave! You'll always be verified in my book!

Verify your site with Google

Carry out the following steps to verify your site with Google:

1. Go to `http://www.google.com/webmasters/tools` and sign in using your Google account.

2. Type the URL of your web site in the empty box, named **Dashboard**, and click on **Add Site**. Your site is now added and it needs to be verified.

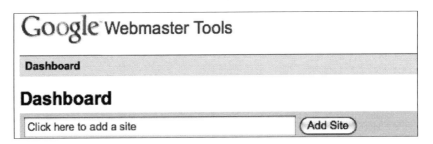

3. Click on the **Verify** link, located next to your site name, as shown in the following screenshot:

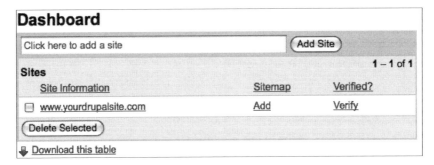

4. Under the **Choose verification method...** option, select **Upload an HTML file**.

 You could also chose **Add a meta tag** and the Site verification module can handle that as well. Either way works equally well.

5. Copy the filename provided, as shown in the following screenshot:

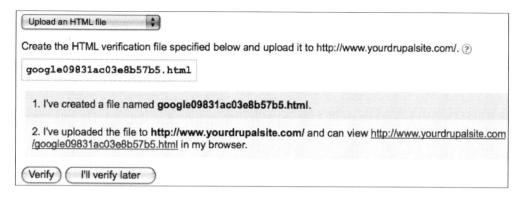

6. Now, install the Site verification module. Refer to the earlier part of this chapter for the step-by-step module installation instructions.

7. Go to `http://www.yourDrupalsite.com/admin/build/site-verify/add/google`. You'll see a screen similar to the following screenshot:

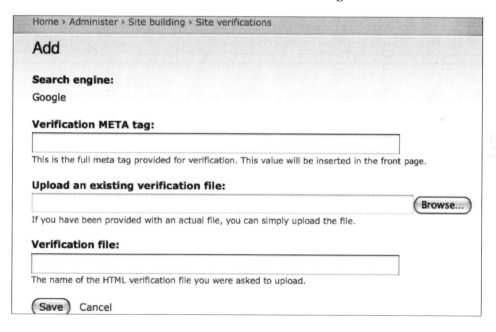

8. In the **Verification file** field, paste in the filename that you got from Google and click on the **Save** button.

9. Test the URL. In your browser, open the following link:
    `http://www.yourDrupalsite.com/<nameofspecialGooglefile.html>`.
    You'll be able to see a screen similar to the following screenshot:

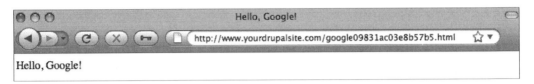

10. Go back to Google Webmaster Tools and click on the **Verify** button.
    In a few seconds, you should see the success message, as shown in the
    following screenshot:

Google Webmaster Tools settings

Now that your site is verified with Google, you can take advantage of all the great
features that Google Webmaster Tools has to offer. Here are a few to which you
should pay particular attention.

Preferred domain

Depending on how you set up your `.htaccess` file (refer to Chapter 7, *robots.txt,
.htaccess, and W3C Validation*), you can access your Drupal site using a www or not.
For example, `http://www.yourDrupalsite.com/` or `http://yourDrupalsite.com/` both will point to the front page of your site. This is not ideal because Google
may treat those two URLs as two different pages and assume they contain totally
different content. You'd actually be competing with yourself in Google and that's not
a good thing.

Fortunately, you can fix this problem using the preferred domain setting.
The preferred domain is the one that you would like used to index your site's
pages and to have show up in Google. If you specify your preferred domain as
`http://www.yourDrupalsite.com` and Google finds a link to your site that is
formatted as `http://yourDrupalsite.com`, they'll treat that link as if it was
`http://www.yourDrupalsite.com`. In addition, Google will take your preference
into account when displaying URLs in the search results.

Set a preferred domain in Google Webmaster Tools

To set a preferred domain in Google Webmaster Tools carry out the following steps:

1. On the Webmaster Tools Dashboard, click the URL for your Drupal site.

2. Click on **Settings**, present on the left hand menu.

3. In the **Preferred domain** section, select the option of your choice, and then click on **Save**, as shown in the following screenshot:

> **Does it matter, which one?**
>
> No, not really. You can choose either www or non-www— there is no advantage between the two. However, you should pick one. If you don't specify Google may split the value of the incoming links to your site between the two options, which will lower your overall ranking.

Crawl rate

If you are on a slow server, you may want to consider asking Google to be a bit more considerate about how much data it grabs from your site at a time. This is called the **crawl rate**. It doesn't effect how often Google visits, just how many pages they ask for at a time. It can be very helpful if you're experiencing a server slowdown.

Setting the crawl rate in Google Webmaster Tools

Carry out the following steps in order to set the crawl rate in Google Webmaster Tools:

1. On the Webmaster Tools Dashboard, click the URL for your Drupal site.

2. Click **Settings** from the left hand menu.

3. In the **Crawl rate** section, select **Set custom crawl rate**.

4. Adjust the slider to change the crawl rate, as shown in the following screenshot:

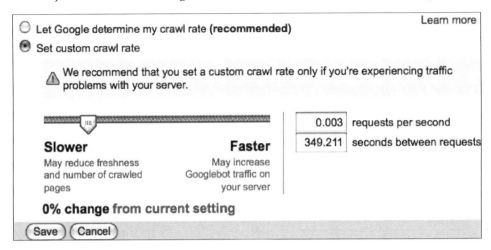

5. Finally, click on **Save**.

Understanding search engine crawlers

Did you ever wonder how all those pages got into the search engines in the first place? There's a magic search engine genie that flies from server to server waving a magic wand; not really but close. Actually, there is a computer program called a **crawler** (or sometimes a **spider** or **robot** or **'bot**) that lives on the search engine's servers. Its job is to surf the Web and save anything it finds. It starts by visiting sites that it already knows about and after that, follows any links that it finds along the way. At each site that it visits, it grabs all the HTML code from every single page it can find and saves that on its own servers.

Later, an indexing server will take that HTML code, examine it, parse it, filter it, analyze it, and some other secret stuff (a lot like waving that magic wand). Finally, your site is saved into the search engine's index. Now, it's finally ready to be served up as a search result. Total time elapsed? About two minutes.

One important thing to note here is that search engine crawlers follow the same links that you do. That means that if you can't click the link, then there's a good chance that the crawler can't click the link either. Fortunately Google does a great job of following JavaScript links, but if you're using JavaScript for your Drupal navigation menus then chances are good that other search engines can't see much past your front page. That's where some creative techniques can really come in handy. **Breadcrumbs** to show navigation or an XML sitemap (refer to Chapter 5, *Sitemaps*) can help the crawler find out where to go next. That's why those tools are sometimes called **spider food**.

Paid tools

Here are a handful of useful tools that are not quite free. They are useful and have a place in every good SEO bag of tricks.

CrazyEgg

Eye-tracking studies show you where people are looking while they're on your web site. Dries Buytart, the founder of Drupal, showed one during his 2008 **State of Drupal** address at the Boston DrupalCon. The heat map shows where the users look in the first five seconds after landing on Drupal's main administration page. The red X's show where the users clicked, as shown in the following screenshot:

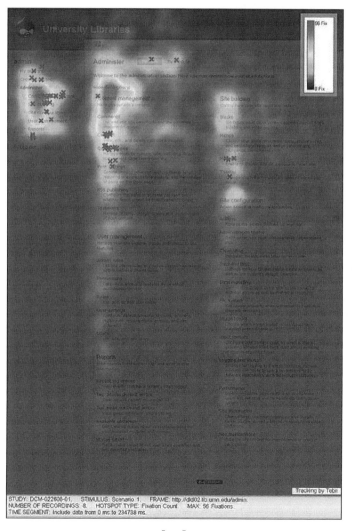

With CrazyEgg, you can do something similar on your own web site. Although it can't track your visitors' eye movements, it can show a heat map that shows you where your visitors click. This is another one of those tools that you should install and let run for a few weeks or months so that you can collect some useful data.

The Crazy Egg tool costs $9 per month. To try it yourself, visit their website at `www.CrazyEgg.com`.

Mint

Mint is an extensible, self-hosted web site analytics program. Visits, referrers, popular pages, and searches can all be taken in at a glance on Mint's flexible dashboard. It's not as powerful as Google Analytics but it's very simple to use and hosted right on your own site, so it's fast and timely. The following screenshot shows how the Mint tool works:

Mint costs $30 per site. To try it yourself, visit their website at `www.haveamint.com`.

Other Great Tools

There are several other great free tools you can use. Let's go ahead and have a look at them.

Installing two browsers

Why would I possibly need two browsers? One of the great features of Drupal is that it knows if you're logged in and will show different screens when you're the admin of the site than it would if you're an anonymous visitor. For example, you may have noticed an **Edit** link on each node of your site when you're logged in as the admin.

This little trick is cookie-based. Browsers don't share cookies so you can be logged in to your site on Firefox and show up as an anonymous user in Safari. With two browsers installed, you can make changes as the admin on one browser and see those changes as an anonymous visitor on the other.

Google Toolbar

Another helpful tool is the **Google Toolbar**. Google Toolbar gives you some very helpful tools like a Google search box and the Google Pagerank indicator. Visit any page on the web and the toolbar will tell you the Pagerank of that page. Currently, the Google Toolbar only supports Firefox and Internet Explorer. The following screenshot shows the Google Toolbar for Mozilla Firefox:

PageRank

PageRank is a very important factor which needs to be taken into consideration for the Search Engine Optimization of your site.

What is it?

PageRank is a number between zero and ten that expresses Google's view of the importance of a web page. Important pages receive higher PageRank and are more likely to appear at the top of search results. Links pass PageRank value from one page to another. It's sometimes called **link juice**. A link from an important site passes more link juice than a link from a lesser site.

How do I get more?

You can get more PageRank simply by having pages with PageRank link to you. Each page that links to your site, passes a little of its PageRank to your site. The more links you have and the higher the PageRank of the sites that link to you the more PageRank you get.

SEO for Firefox plugin

Assuming that you're using Firefox, adding the SEO for Firefox plugin to your browser will add a plethora of great SEO-related tools to use right in your browser. When you view search results in Google, this nifty plugin overlays useful data about each site in the results. For example, it will show you the PageRank, domain age, and how many backlinks it has, as well as how many links from popular web sites like dmoz, twitter, del.icio.us, and Digg. This can be invaluable when you're doing keyword research (refer to Chapter 2, *Keyword Research*). Download it from the following link: `http://budURL.com/seoforfirefox`.

Yahoo! site explorer

Google isn't the only search engine that offers some great tools. Yahoo! is one of the few search engines that will provide you with a list of all the links you have coming into your site. Just point your browser at `http://siteexplorer.search.yahoo.com/` and put in your URL. You can even add a badge to your site that tells you how many in links you have, as shown in the following screenshot:

Summary

In this chapter, we covered all the tools you're going to need for Drupal SEO. From Drupal and all the great modules available for SEO to setting up a Google account, this chapter is the foundational to the rest of this book. At this point, you should have:

- A Drupal site set up and installed
- A good grasp of how to install a Drupal module
- The SEO Checklist module installed
- A Google account
- A Google Analytics account
- A Google Webmaster Tools account
- A preferred domain and crawl rate set in Google
- Two browsers installed
- The Google Toolbar and the SEO for Firefox plugin.

In the next chapter, we explore keyword research—the most fundamentally important part of your SEO campaign.

2
Keyword Research

SEO is necessary—you've got to do it if you want to rank well for keywords. Simple in concept, keywords are actually very complicated things. They bring order to chaos, define markets, and reveal intent. Keyword data simultaneously tells you how many people are looking for your product or service and what those people will do once they find you. The results of a keyword search can tell you who the top people are in an industry and inform you of upcoming trends in the market. Keywords are the most visible focal point of free market competition between business interests. Search engine optimization is a popularity contest for **keywords** and this is a popularity contest you want to win.

The most critical part of an SEO project is finding the right keywords. You will spend months working on your web site, getting links, and telling the world that your site is the authority on that keyword. It's critical that when you finally arrive, your customers are there to embrace you. If you pick the wrong keywords, you'll spend months working only to find that there is nobody who wants to buy your product. Ouch! An extra few hours researching your keywords in the beginning will help you avoid this fate.

In this chapter, we're going to explore:

- What is a keyword and why it matters
- Why keyword research is perhaps the most important thing you'll do in an SEO campaign
- Setting goals for your keywords
- How to use your site to find great keywords including installing and configuring the Top Searches module
- Several external keyword research tools to speed up the process of finding the best terms
- A walk-through of the keyword research process

What a keyword is

Keywords are many things to many people. For the purpose of this SEO campaign, there are really only two things about keywords that we need to understand to get the job done. Keywords aggregate searchers into organized groups and a keyword defines a market.

> **Keywords** are single words that a search engine user types into the search box to try to find what they're looking for. **Key phrases** are the same as keywords except for the fact that they consist of two or more words. For the sake of simplicity, throughout this book let's use keywords to mean both, keywords and key phrases.

Keywords aggregate searchers into organized groups

Millions of random people visit Google every day. When they arrive, they are amorphous—a huddled mass yearning for enlightenment with nothing more than a blank Google search form to guide them. As each person types keywords into Google and clicks the **Search** button, this random mass of people becomes extraordinarily organized. Each keyword identifies exactly what that person is looking for and allows Google to show them results that would satisfy their query.

Much like a labor union, the more searchers there are looking for a particular phrase, the more clout they have with the businesses who want to sell to them. However, instead of more pay and better health benefits, you get better search results. If there are a thousand people per month looking for keyword A and a hundred people per month looking for keyword B, then chances are good that there are more competitors focused on keyword A. More competition means better optimization is required to show up at the top. Better optimization requires more content, closer attention to meeting the needs of the group, and more interesting web sites.

A keyword defines a market

This organization of searchers is what gives Google such power. In a very real way, Google creates billions of tiny markets every day. There is a buyer (the searcher) looking for a product, the seller (the web site owners) selling what they've got, and the middleman (Google) organizing everything and facilitating the transaction. The transaction takes place when the searcher clicks on the result of a keyword search and is whisked off to the seller's web site. However, it doesn't always go smoothly.

In fact, very high percentages of the time the searcher doesn't find what they're looking for so they hit the back button and try again. They may try a different result on the same page or type in a different keyword and do the entire search again. Each time you have an opportunity to convince them that yours is the right site with the best information and most promising solution to their questions. It is in your best interest to provide a web site that quickly engages the searchers, pulls them in, and keeps the dialogue going.

Why keyword research is important

As a Drupal site owner, you have the opportunity to position yourself as the best site available for the keywords people are searching for.

Know thy customer

There are hundreds of good marketing books out there to help you better understand your audience. All that good information applies to SEO as well. The better you know your audience, the better you can guess what keywords they are typing in Google to find companies like yours.

You're an expert in your field, so of course you know many of the keywords that people use to find your products and services. But, are you sure you know them all?

A few years ago Tom, a friend of mine, hired me to do SEO for his high-end landscaping firm. His company designs and installs yards, trees, retaining walls, and so on, outside million dollar homes in the hill country near Austin, Texas. We sat down in an early morning meeting and he said, "Ben, the right keyword is landscaping. I know it so there's no reason to do all this research. Don't waste your time and my money. Just do landscaping and that's that". Being the thorough person that I am, I did the keyword research anyway. Guess what I found?

The number one phrase in his business was landscaping. However, a very close second was landscaper. And, while landscaping had dozens of competitors—some of them were very well entrenched—there were only a handful of competitors showing up for landscaper.

The next day, I called Tom and told him what I found. "You know what?" he said, "Now that you mention it, many of our customers do refer to us as landscapers—'I need a landscaper. Call a landscaper' ".

So, we started his campaign targeting the keyword **landscaper**. Because there was so little competition, he ranked in the top five in a matter of weeks and was number one in Google within two months. He was dominating half the search traffic within two months! The leads were rolling in so we switched to the keyword **landscaping**. It took longer—about three months—for him to break into the top ten. By that time, he had so many inquiries, he hardly even noticed.

The lesson here is three-fold:

1. You may know some of the keywords, however, that doesn't mean you know them all.
2. Just because you think of yourself in one particular way doesn't mean your customers do.
3. By taking the time to do keyword research, you will reveal opportunities in your market that you didn't know existed.

What your keyword goal is

Before you start looking at keywords, you need to fix your goal firmly in your mind. There are basically two major reasons to do SEO.

Goal 1: Brand awareness

This may come as a surprise but there are people out there who don't know that you exist. SEO is a powerful and inexpensive way to get your name out there and build some credibility with your target customers. There are three major types of brand awareness:

Company brand awareness

Company brand awareness works on getting the name of your company into the market. If you want to build credibility for Big Computers Unlimited as a whole, then you probably want a campaign focused on getting your company listed where other top producers of PCs are listed. PC, computer, or fast computer all might be good terms.

Product brand awareness

Product brand awareness focuses on building general market knowledge of one product or line of products that your company produces. If you work for Big Computers Unlimited and you want to sell more Intergalactic Gamer brand computers at retail stores throughout the country, then you probably want to build a campaign around keywords like **Gaming PC** or even **high-end PC**.

Credibility

A 2004 survey by iProspect found that two out of three search engine users believed that the highest search results in Google were the top brands for their industry; there is little reason to believe this perception has changed. That means that just by being at the top of Google will gain you a certain level of trust among search engine users. If Big Computers Unlimited can rank in the top three for Gaming PCs, they'll develop a lot of creed among gamers.

Goal 2: Conversions

Conversions are a fancy way of saying that the visitor did what you wanted them to do. There are three typical types of conversions:

Transactional

A transaction is just what it sounds like. Someone puts in a credit card and buys your product. This is typical of most product-focused web sites but isn't limited to this narrow category. Your web site may sell registrations to online training, subscriptions to magazines, or even credit monitoring. The bottom line is that it can be purchased on the site. You need to focus your keyword research on terms that will bring buyers who are ready to purchase right now. Words like buy, price, merchant, store, and shop indicate a desire for immediate purchase.

Give them the transactional information they need like price, color choices, size, quantity discounts, return policy, and delivery options. With this information and a great checkout experience you'll have them buying from you in no time.

Ubercart
Ubercart is simply the best shopping cart solution for Drupal.
If you're a transactional web site and you need an e-commerce solution, start here: http://www.ubercart.org/.

Lead Generation

If you're in an industry with a long sales cycle like real estate, legal services, or medical, then you're probably interested in generating leads rather than online transactions. If you sell a service or product that requires direct contact with your customer, like consulting or personal training, then you probably want leads too.

Lead generation means that instead of buying from your web site, you're interested in someone expressing an interest in doing business with you so that you can follow up with them later. You let them express interest by filling out a contact form, emailing you, or even picking up the phone and calling you. You need to focus your keyword research on terms that will bring people who are perhaps a little earlier in the buying process. Words like review, compare, best, information, and generic names of your product indicate a user is researching but not quite ready to buy. You'll need to provide a lot of information on your web site to inform them and shape their thinking about your product.

Page impression (or ad impression)

Some web sites make money when visitors view an ad. To these sites, a conversion may simply be someone clicking on one or more pages so that they'll see one more ads. You need to focus your keyword research on terms that will bring people seeking information or news to your web site.

Keyword research tools

There are many tools to help you find the right keywords. It's not important that you use them all but you should try a few of them just so you can see what's out there. Here are my favorites in order of preference:

Your own web site

The most important keyword research tool at your disposal is your own web site, `http://www.yourDrupalsite.com/`. If you already have some traffic, chances are that they're coming from somewhere. With analytics installed, you should be able to find out what they're searching on with just a few clicks. If you have Google Analytics installed then you can easily see this data by logging in to its admin section and then going to **Traffic Sources | Search Engines | Google**.

This information can be invaluable if you cross-reference it with your current positions in the search engines. Say, for example, that you're getting 100 searchers a month on a term that you're on page 2 of Google. That's a good indicator that people are searching hard to find a company like yours and that may be a very good term to focus on with your search engine campaign. If you're getting that much traffic on page 2, imagine if you were in the top three on page 1.

Drupal has a built-in search engine—another great tool to see what the people are searching for, after they've already visited your site. There's an insanely useful module for that, called Top Searches (`http://drupal.org/project/top_searches`) that does a better job that Drupal's built-in list. This module was developed by the founder of Linnovate, Zohar Stolar. Thanks, Zohar!

How to set up the Top Searches module

Carry out the following steps to set up Top Searches module:

1. Download the latest version: `http://drupal.org/project/top_searches`.

2. Install the module like you would any Drupal module (see Chapter 1) and enable it.

3. Visit `http://www.yourDrupalsite.com/admin/settings/top_searches` or go to your admin screen and click on **Administer | Site Configuration | Top Searches** link. You should a screen similar to the following screenshot:

4. Set the option **Should counters be presented next to the items in the block?** to **Yes** and click on **Save configuration**.

5. To view the searches, you need to set up a block. Set up the block by going to `http://www.yourDrupalsite.com/admin/build/block` and clicking on **Configure**, located next to the **Top Searches** listing.

6. Let's make this block only visible to authenticated users and only on the admin screen.

7. Under **Role specific visibility settings**, select **authenticated user**.

8. Under **Page specific visibility settings**, click on **Show on only the listed pages** and add `admin` under **Pages:**. You should end up with something like this:

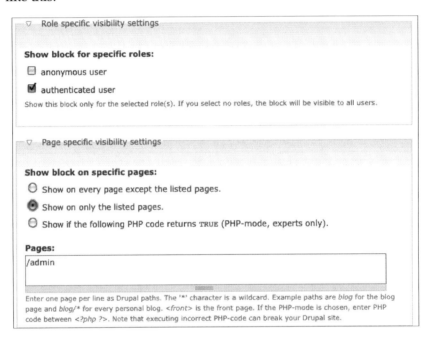

9. Click on the **Save** block and go to the admin page and you will see your **Top Searches** block.

It may take some time for it to fully populate with data. Now that you've got some data from your own site, let's take a look at some external tools for keyword research.

Your competition

How your SEO-savvy competitors market themselves can reveal a lot to you about where your customers are. If they've optimized, you can easily see what terms they consider important, just by visiting their web site.

How to scrape your competitors' web site for keywords

There are two ways to scrape your competitors' web site for keywords:

The quick way

Carry out the following steps to scrape your competitors' web site for keywords using the quick way:

1. Go to your competitor's web site.
2. Click **View Source** in your browser.
3. Look for the keywords Metatag. It looks like this: `<meta name="keywords" content="some keywords here">`.

The easy way:

Carry out the following steps to scrape your competitors' web site for keywords using the easy way:

1. Use Google Adwords Keyword Tool.
2. Select **Web site Content** and enter your competitors' web site.
3. Review results.

You don't want to get too carried away with this. If all you're doing is getting your competitors keywords then you'll miss those great niches of opportunity that you'll find doing the full research. Still, it's a great way to kick start your keyword hunt.

Google Adwords Keyword Tool

Visit `https://adwords.google.com/select/KeywordToolExternal` to check the Google Adwords Keyword Tool.

The Google Adwords Keyword Tool shows how many people searched for a particular keyword and related keywords in the last month or so. At its most basic, you type in the keyword you're interested in and it gives you the quantity of searches for that keyword and derivatives of that keyword.

Why would Google just give this information away? Google makes their money when businesses buy ads. In the Google Adwords Keyword Tool, they've created an excellent resource to help advertisers find highly trafficked keywords for their campaigns. Luckily, this tool is free, even if you aren't going to advertise.

Apart from being free, there are several advantages to Google Adwords Keyword Tool.

It is Google's own data, so you can count on it being accurate for 60-70% of search engine users. If you're focused on Google, this is the tool to use. Period!

It gives you an exhaustive list of terms. If you type in your main term, it will often produce hundreds of additional, related terms for you to consider. Some other free tools will only give you ten at a time which makes research a very time-intensive process.

It allows you to filter results using negative keywords. So, if you sell software, you might use the negative keywords **-free**, **-crack**, **-serial** to filter out all the people who are looking for free, cracked, or just want a serial number. That will make a huge difference to the resulting volume count.

Other helpful things include the ability to download the resulting list as a CSV, using your web site (or even a competitor's web site) to start the keyword search, and the ability to match the results based on broad, phrase, or exact.

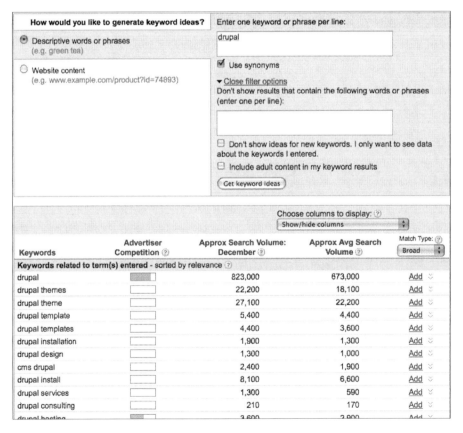

Google Zeitgeist

Visit `http://www.google.com/zeitgeist` to check out the Google Zeitgeist web site.

Zeitgeist is German for **time ghost** or **the spirit of our times**. The idea that there are certain thoughts or ideas that make their way through society. Google Zeitgeist shows you emerging trends by showing the fastest rising search phrases in a given time period in each of four major services: search, news, images, and book search. You can also see things like **Top of Mind**, **Politics**, and **Trendsetters**.

For example, the **2008 USA Year-End Google Zeitgeist** shows that the fastest growing terms in search are **obama**, **facebook**, **att**, and **iphone**. So, how does this help you with keywords research? It can help you to take advantage of trends in your markets. If you can somehow tie your products to the major trends, then you can take advantage of huge amounts of traffic.

2008 Year-End Google Zeitgeist

After a whirlwind year of election news, economy woes, and the lead-up to the showstopping Summer Games in Beijing, we're looking back to see what was on the minds of Americans through it all. One thing's for sure: it was a wild ride.

"Fastest rising" means we looked at the most popular searches conducted for 11 months of 2008 (we compile this list by early December) and ranked them based on how much their frequency increased compared to 2007.

Google.com - Fastest Rising (U.S.)

1. obama
2. facebook
3. att
4. iphone
5. youtube
6. fox news
7. palin
8. beijing 2008
9. david cook
10. surf the channel

Google News - Fastest Rising (U.S.)

1. sarah palin
2. american idol
3. mccain
4. olympics
5. ike (hurricane)

Google Trends

Visit `http://www.google.com/trends` to check out the Google Trends web site.

Google Trends allows you to see how a keyword has done over the years. For example, remember that kid who sang the Numa Numa song on YouTube? Well, his popularity is waning (finally!). Check it out:

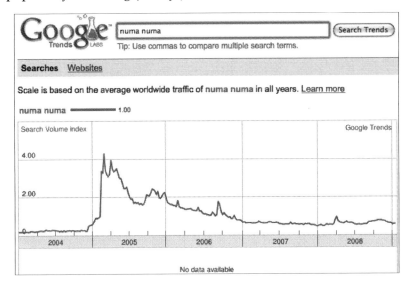

Google Trends even lets you compare two different words to see which one has more traffic. With some comparisons, it even charts major news stories to drops or peaks in traffic:

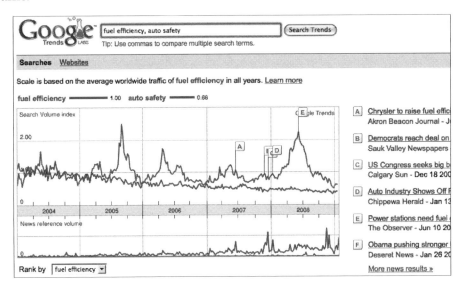

SEOmoz

Visit `http://budurl.com/seom` to check out the SEOmoz web site.

SEOmoz offers a suite of free and paid **Pro** tools to help your optimization efforts. For example, their **Term Extractor** tool will tell you what keywords your competition is optimizing for. When I put in Amazon.com, I got gems such as **books** and **gift cards**. No surprises there. Other great tools include:

- **Keyword Difficulty**: It tells you how hard it will be to achieve ranking for a particular keyword
- **Popular Searches**: It aggregates and archives popular searches from various sources
- **Juicy Link Finder**: It finds links that have authority—old domains with a high PageRank that rank well for the keyword you enter

They seem to add new tools every month. At $79 per month, this is not cheap. Try it at least once and decide for yourself if the Pro membership is worth it. I'm a paying subscriber.

Keyword Discovery

Visit `http://budurl.com/KeywordDiscovery` to check out the Keyword Discovery web site.

Suppose you want to know what's going on outside of Google—non-Google searches do make up 30-40% of the market. And, say you want to see monthly trends for your keywords and create campaigns that you can come back to and revise over time. Well, pry open your wallet and head on over to Keyword Discovery. Their free tool just isn't as good as Google's, however, for a reasonable monthly fee you get an excellent keyword research tool.

The best thing about Keyword Discovery is that you have an account that you can log in to and save your research. This is great if you are running several campaigns across different sites or you just don't have time to do all your research in one fell swoop. Also, their related terms finder is second to none—even better than Google's in some cases. They show data from all over the Web too by capturing data from many sources, including ISPs and search logs from large web sites (they don't reveal which ones, though). A worthy research tool in your kit.

WordTracker

Visit `http://budurl.com/WordTrackerFreeTrial` to check out the WordTracker web site.

WordTracker has been around the longest for good reason. They provide dozens of tools to help you find the best keywords. They gather their data from Meta search engines—search engines that aggregate search results from many different search engines. They then extrapolate the number of searches on a particular term based on market share data. It's not perfect but it does provide some great data points.

One of the most helpful features is the step-by-step wizards which walk you through your keyword research. If you're new to keyword research, this feature alone is worth the membership fee. The price is quite reasonable when you consider that you can get a fully-functioning seven day trial for free! If you're just doing one web site, sign up for the trial, get your research done, and cancel it. I like free.

How to pick the best keywords

By now, you know the goals of your SEO campaign—branding, lead generation, sales transactions, and so on. Now, it's time to dig into the data. There are infinite number of ways to go about doing keyword research. I'm going to take you step-by-step through one of them. It's not necessarily the right or the best way but it's a good, solid technique that I've used many times to produce excellent results.

You need one more thing—a spreadsheet. Whether you use Excel, Numbers, or Google Docs, the easiest way to keep track of a list of keywords is in a huge spreadsheet. It doesn't have to be complicated, just a simple list of keywords and some key data about each one. Something like this:

Keyword Research

Keyword	Searched	Source	Difficulty	Rank	Keep?
...	...	...			...

Google's list

Google will tempt you into adding all the keywords to a list that they'll keep for you and then you can download when you're done. I avoid this for two reasons. First, they only save the keyword, not how many searches it brought so the data is incomplete. Second, it can sometimes take me a few hours or even days to finish my keyword research. Google doesn't save the data for that long so I might have to start all over if I forgot to export it. It's better to just build your own spreadsheet from the get go.

The scenario

Let's say that I'm doing keyword research for a large computer manufacturer called Big Computers Unlimited. They sell computers all over the U.S. from their web site and a few select retail outlets. They recently acquired a smaller competitor called Intergalactic Gaming that specialized in high-end gaming PCs. The purpose of this campaign is to create more online sales of the specialized line of entertainment computers by increasing traffic from the search engines. While Big Computers spends millions each year on search marketing, this campaign is a trial to test the waters so they've only allocated a few thousand dollars over the course of three months.

How to gather a keywords list

Carry out the following steps to gather a keywords list:

1. Visit `https://adwords.google.com/select/KeywordToolExternal`. You'll start with the most basic keyword that you can think of, for your industry, like **pc**, and click **Get keyword ideas**; as shown in the following screenshot:

2. It's a good idea to adjust your match type to phrase or even exact since SEO typically focuses on a single, specific keyword at a time.

Broad, Phrase, Exact: What do they mean? Say you want the term **tennis shoe**. Broad Match is the outcome of any possible search that contains your keywords, including searches that had other words in them, plural versions of your keywords, and even synonyms. For example: **shoes for tennis**, **tennis shoes**, or **tennis sneaker** would match. Phrase Match can include other terms as long as it includes the exact phrase you've specified. For example: **nike tennis shoes** fits but **shoes for tennis** would not. Exact Match means that the phrase must match exactly. For example: **tennis shoes** and nothing else.

3. Click on **Approx Avg Search Volume** to sort the list of keywords that was generated by searching for the term **pc**. This shows you the most searched keywords at the top.

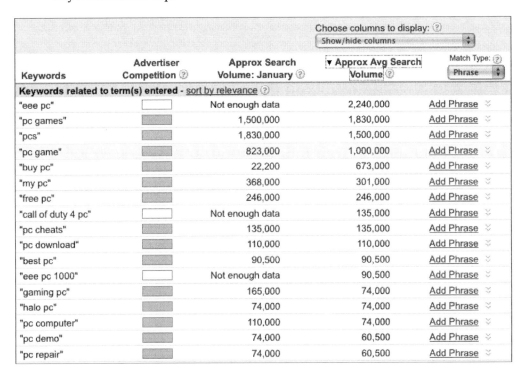

Keywords	Advertiser Competition ⑦	Approx Search Volume: January ⑦	▼ Approx Avg Search Volume ⑦	Match Type: ⑦ Phrase
Keywords related to term(s) entered - sort by relevance ⑦				
"eee pc"		Not enough data	2,240,000	Add Phrase ⌄
"pc games"		1,500,000	1,830,000	Add Phrase ⌄
"pcs"		1,830,000	1,500,000	Add Phrase ⌄
"pc game"		823,000	1,000,000	Add Phrase ⌄
"buy pc"		22,200	673,000	Add Phrase ⌄
"my pc"		368,000	301,000	Add Phrase ⌄
"free pc"		246,000	246,000	Add Phrase ⌄
"call of duty 4 pc"		Not enough data	135,000	Add Phrase ⌄
"pc cheats"		135,000	135,000	Add Phrase ⌄
"pc download"		110,000	110,000	Add Phrase ⌄
"best pc"		90,500	90,500	Add Phrase ⌄
"eee pc 1000"		Not enough data	90,500	Add Phrase ⌄
"gaming pc"		165,000	74,000	Add Phrase ⌄
"halo pc"		74,000	74,000	Add Phrase ⌄
"pc computer"		110,000	74,000	Add Phrase ⌄
"pc demo"		74,000	60,500	Add Phrase ⌄
"pc repair"		74,000	60,500	Add Phrase ⌄

4. Looks daunting, doesn't it? Don't worry, you're just gathering ideas for now. Notice that there are a lot of phrases that have words that are completely off-topic, like **free** or **repair**? Well it's time to filter those out. Click the **Filter my results** link, located just below the keyword box. Enter one negative keyword per line, as shown in the following screenshot:

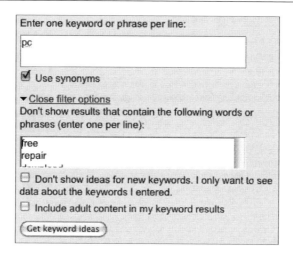

5. Click on **Get keyword ideas**. Now the list is a bit cleaner. Nice!

6. Notice that there are quite a few phrases related to games, like **pc games**, **pc game**, and **gaming pc**. They might seem like great choices but stop to consider that someone who is looking for **pc games** is not the same as someone who is looking to buy a high-end games pc. Careful! Google treats the search phrase **games pc** and **pc games** as the same in this result. If you change the **Match Type** to **Exact**, the number of results drops in half. Let's find out how many of those terms are actually games pc.

7. Go back up to the keyword phrase list and type in **games pc**, **gaming pc**, and **game pc**. Under **Filter my results**, check the box next to **Don't show ideas for new keywords**. This will just show you results for those three terms. Now click on **Get Keyword Ideas**.

8. Change the **Match Type** to **Exact** and you'll see a very different story:

Keywords	Advertiser Competition ⑦	Approx Search Volume: January ⑦	▼ Approx Avg Search Volume ⑦	Match Type: ⑦ Exact ⬍
Keywords related to term(s) entered - sort by relevance ⑦				
[gaming pc]	▮▮▮	27,100	27,100	Add Exact ⌄
[games pc]	▮▮▮	3,600	3,600	Add Exact ⌄
[game pc]	▮▮▮	2,400	2,900	Add Exact ⌄

9. These are still terms that should be considered but they're certainly not as hot as you may have thought at first. Add each phrase and it's search data to your spreadsheet.

10. Now, let's unclick the **Don't show ideas...** box and see what we get. There are some good ones here: **gaming pc**, **best gaming pc**, **gamer pc**, **video game pc**, and so on. I'll add them all to my spreadsheet. This could go on for hours and for a large project, it's not unusual to have a list of 500 keywords after a few hours of research.

11. Now, let's find out how hard it's going to be to rank for those terms. Notice that there's a column on the report called **Advertiser Competition**. That report will tell you how many advertisers are bidding on that key phrase in Google's Adwords. That doesn't exactly correspond to how many are trying to rank for that term organically but it's probably close, so let's use it.

12. Hover your mouse over each **Advertiser Competition** bar and a little pop-up will give you an indication of how difficult it is. For example, next to **games pc** it says **Very high advertiser competition**. Since I will probably want to sort the list, I'll change that into a number; say 10 for the hardest and 0 for no competition.

13. After doing all that, my spreadsheet looks similar to the following screenshot:

keyword	searched	source	Difficulty	Current Rank	Keep?
best gaming pc	3600	Google	10		
game pc	74000	Google	10		
gamer pc	6600	Google	9		
games pc	135000	Google	10		
gaming pc	74000	Google	10		
gaming pcs	8100	Google	10		
video game pc	3600	Google	8		

14. Now, let's find out where Big Computers already ranks for these terms. We put each term into Google and here's what we find:

keyword	searched	source	Difficulty	Current Rank	Keep?
best gaming pc	3600	Google	10	NR	
game pc	74000	Google	10	19	
gamer pc	6600	Google	9	NR	
games pc	135000	Google	10	92	
gaming pc	74000	Google	10	43	
gaming pcs	8100	Google	10	NR	
video game pc	3600	Google	8	NR	

Picking the right terms

Now, we've got some decisions to make. There are some huge terms on that list with over 100,000 searchers per month and very high competition. However, there are two terms that Big Computers already ranks for: **game pc**, **games pc** and **gaming pc**. All three have considerable traffic but notice that they rank on page 2 for **game pc**. With 74,000 searches per month, this is a hot term and definitely makes our short list.

The term **gamer pc** has somewhat less competition as does **video game pc**. Although there's relatively little traffic, less competition means an easier time getting ranked. We'll keep both of these for now. On the other hand, **best gaming pc** and **gaming pcs** have high competition and low traffic. We'll reject both terms for our initial campaign but they might be good to add in later. That leaves **games pc** and **gaming pc**—both terms are high traffic and high competition. If this was a full campaign, I think they'd make the list—remember, though, that this is just a trial. Since we want to justify a fuller campaign, we need some easy wins. We already have three good terms to work with, so I'll say no to these final two terms. So, my almost-final spreadsheet looks similar to the following screenshot:

keyword	searched	source	Difficulty	Current Rank	Keep?
best gaming pc	3600	Google	10	NR	no
game pc	74000	Google	10	19	yes
gamer pc	6600	Google	9	NR	yes
games pc	135000	Google	10	92	no
gaming pc	74000	Google	10	43	no
gaming pcs	8100	Google	10	NR	no
video game pc	3600	Google	8	NR	yes

Getting rid of the wrong terms

At least as important as finding the right terms is rejecting terms that are not right. Some terms seem perfect until you put them under the microscope, then you will start to see the flaws in your own logic. Here are a few steps you can follow to make sure you've got good keywords:

1. Google the keyword and look at the results. Do you see relevant results?

2. Use Wikipedia to read about your keywords. Are those words used in other ways in a different industry than yours?

3. Ask your customers, colleagues, and companions: "What does <keyword> mean to you?"

4. Look in the \<gasp\> phone book. What companies show up for the phrase you're evaluating? Are they the right kinds of companies?

5. If you've got some money to spend, try running an Adwords campaign. Put in all your keywords and write some ads. After a few weeks, you should have a pretty definitive idea of which terms perform the best for you.

Now that we've got our keywords, it's time to start using them on our web site.

Summary

In this chapter, we covered the tools you're going to need to do keyword research, from Drupal stats in your own web site to all the great tools available online. Keyword research is one of the most important things you'll do in SEO so make sure you've taken the time to do it right. At this point, you should have:

- A good understanding of the goals that you've set for your web site
- The Top Searches module installed
- A working knowledge of at least one of the keyword research tools—probably Google's tool
- A list of the keywords that will be the focus of your SEO campaign

In the next chapter, we starting putting those keywords to use on your Drupal web site

3
On-Page Optimization

Google and the other search engines look at the content of your site to determine whether you should show up for a particular search. It makes sense. If you don't even mention the keyword, then you probably aren't talking about that topic. It's like picking up a book and skimming the title, chapter titles, headings, text, and appendices to find out what it's about. If you're looking for a book on Drupal and you don't see the word Drupal mentioned anywhere, chances are it's not a Drupal book. Google basically does the same thing with your web site. If the keyword doesn't appear anywhere on your site, they won't rank you for that keyword.

The first step in convincing Google that you are the best is to tweak your site so that the keywords show up in all the right places. These changes to your site for the search engines are collectively called **On-Page Optimization**. Thankfully, because you're using Drupal, it's a lot easier than it might be otherwise.

In this chapter, we're going to look at the most important aspects of on page optimization:

- Changing your HTML `<title>` tags with the page title module
- Writing `<title>` tags that Google and your visitors will love
- Setting your web site's name
- Optimizing navigation links
- Making URL paths clean and search engine optimized with the Path and Pathauto modules
- 301 redirects with the Path Redirect module
- Using the Global Redirect module to fix Drupal's duplicate content problems

Page titles

The **page title** (also known as **title tag**) is a line of text in the HTML of a web page, summarizing what that web page is all about. It serves the following functions:

- It tells visitors that they are in the right place
- It is displayed in the browser title bar
- It holds important keywords so that your page can be properly categorized by Google and the other search engines
- It is displayed whenever someone bookmarks your site
- Search engines usually use the page title as the heading of the search results

That's a lot of work for a little blurb of text!

That is why an excellent page title is so important to any good SEO campaign. I may be going out on a limb when I say this, but I believe that the page title is the single most important thing you can do to improve the SEO of your web site.

In practice, the page title is generated by a simple piece of HTML that is placed near the beginning of your html file between the <HEAD> and </HEAD> tags. It looks like this:

```
<HEAD>
<title>Your Drupal Site</title>
</HEAD>
```

Drupal does this automatically for you by using the site name and site slogan of the front page and the node title for individual nodes. For serious SEO tasks, that just doesn't give you the control you need. For example, you might name your node "The 10 Things I like about Austin Real Estate" but you may want to rearrange that for the page title to put the important words first: "Austin Real Estate Top 10 List".

Page title or node title—what's the difference?
In the world of Drupal, the word **title** usually means the title of a node. When you visit a node view, the title is the line of text at the top of the page telling you what that node is called. In the world of HTML, the title is a special piece of code that shows up between <title> and </title> in the header of your web site. Since those worlds collide when you're working on your SEO campaign, it's important to keep those two concepts separate in your mind. Node Title and Page Title, while connected, are two completely different things.

The page title module

The page title module gives you full control of your page titles throughout your site. It lets you:

- Write your own page titles anywhere you can create content
- Define a pattern that will create search engine optimized titles automatically as you create new content

Two active Drupal developers, Nicolas Thompson and John Albin, maintain the Page Title module. We should all doff our hats to them for keeping this module up-to-date. Thanks, guys!

The token module

The page title module uses the token module. **Tokens** are small bits of text that can be called up with simple placeholders, like %site-name or [user]. The token module was a response to the needs of many Drupal developers who found that they were using the same little bits of information again and again in their sites. Examples could be the node title, the day of the week, the site name, and several hundred others. These are all things that are stored in the Drupal database. Before the token module, a developer had to use php code to pull the information out of the database and onto the page.

Now, with the token module, all those little bits of data can be placed into a Drupal site with just a tiny bit of referenced text. The token module doesn't provide any direct functionality itself, it just makes those bits of information available so other modules and users can use them. The token module is co-maintained by Jeff Eaton, Greg Knaddison, and Mike Ryan.

For the Page Title module, tokens will be used to pull information about the current page being displayed and write a nice, search engine optimized title tag. Some typical patterns and their resulting page titles:

- Pattern: **[page-title] | [site-name]**

  Result: **This is my first post | Your Drupal Site**
- Pattern: **I love Drupal by [site-name]**

  Result: **I love Drupal by Your Drupal Site**
- Pattern: **[page-title] - [month] [date], [yyyy]**

  Result: **This is my first post - February 22, 2010**

Before you can use them, however, you'll need to install the token and page title modules.

Installing and configuring the page title module

Carry out the following steps to install it and configure the page title module:

1. Download the Page Title module from `http://drupal.org/project/page_title` and install just like a normal Drupal module. See Chapter 1 for step-by-step module installation instructions. Be sure to install the Token module at the same time: `http://drupal.org/project/token`. Activate both modules at the same time.

2. Point your browser to `http://www.yourDrupalsite.com/admin/content/page_title` or go to your admin screen and click the **Page titles** link. You'll see something similar to the following screenshot:

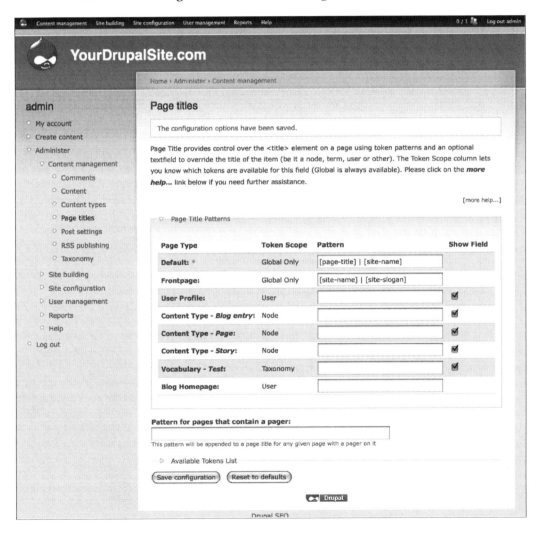

3. Below the pattern fields, you'll see a long **Available Tokens List** that you can copy and paste to create patterns.

 A **token** is a small bit of text related to what's going on at the moment for a visitor to your Drupal site. Examples are the name of the site, the name of the current user, the category that a node is in or even today's date. It lets you use that bit of text in creative ways such as, in this case, creating page titles.

4. Set the patterns you want for the default, front page, and each content type. If you're wondering what pattern to use, skip ahead a few pages where you'll learn how to write great page titles.

5. To the right of each content type, you'll see the **Show Field** checkbox. Deselect the check boxes that you wish, located next to the content types, to be able to control the page title. You probably want to select all of them.

6. Click **Save configuration**.

Rewriting page titles for individual nodes

Sometimes, when you really want to optimize your site properly, you'll need to override the pattern you've set up and tweak your page title for an individual piece of content. Let's look at how to rewrite those patterns on a node-by-node basis.

1. Visit the link `http://www.yourDrupalsite.com/node/add` and create a new piece of content. If you've configured the module properly, you'll notice that the **Create Blog entry** and **Edit Blog entry** screens now have an extra field, called **Page title**.

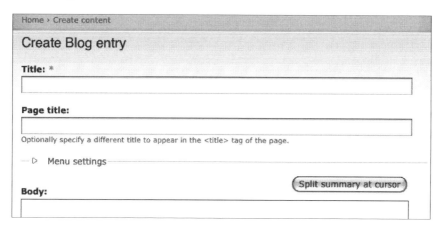

2. Enter some text. If you leave the **Page title** field blank, it will use the pattern you've defined or the default pattern if you haven't created one. If you enter text there, it will override the pattern and display the entered text as the `<title>` of the page.

3. Click on **Save**.

Now, go look at your page in your alternate browser, which will look similar to the following screenshot (note the title at the very top of the browser window):

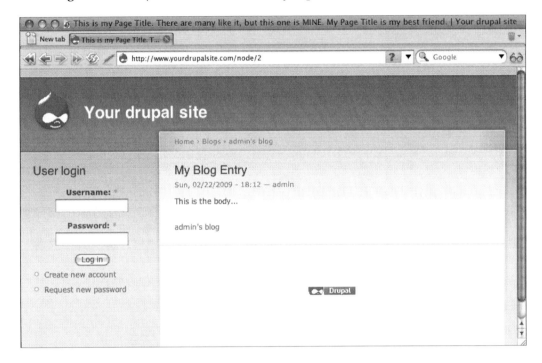

Great! Now that you know how to do it, let's take a look at how to write the best possible page titles for your content.

Rewriting page titles for categories

A new feature of the Page Title module is that you can create specific page titles for taxonomy terms, too. Taxonomy terms can also be called categories. It's very easy. After enabling the Page Title module, you'll see a list of your Taxonomies along with the content types. Tic the **Show Field** box next to the taxonomies (probably all of them) that you want to be able to set the page title. Now, when you edit or create a term in that taxonomy, you'll have a field for the page title.

Writing page titles that Google and your visitors will love

There are two competing forces pulling for your page title's attention. First, the search engines use your page title to help determine where your web site fits. Second, your customers will see and use your page title to help them determine if your site has what they're looking for and to remind them what your site is about when they see it in their bookmark list. A good page title achieves both objectives.

Do you remember, back in Chapter 2, when we did keyword research?

Now is your big chance to put those keywords to work for you. What do people search for when they want what you've got? A very quick example would be a mortgage broker. Obviously, **mortgages** would be a great keyword. But, that's a very competitive term. If the broker only does business in Texas then **Texas Mortgages** would be even better. If that broker wanted to only focus on Austin then **Austin Texas Mortgages** would really narrow the field. Let's work with **Austin Texas Mortgages** as our example term.

So, assuming you've got the best keywords, you just put that as the title and you're done; right? If that's all you did then you'd be fine; however, you'd miss out on the full value that a page title can bring. Let's start with that and see if we can improve on it. Our page title looks like this:

Austin Texas Mortgages

Now, that works for search engines but not so much for customers. Sure, they'll know that you sell mortgages but they may not remember which company. You always want them to remember who you are. So, you could do this:

My Mortgage Co | Austin Texas Mortgages

That's good for your customers; however, it moves the best keywords out of the first position. Search engines assume that the most important words come early in the page title. So, how about this:

Get Austin Texas Mortgages at My Mortgage Co

Well, now you're optimizing for the word **Get**. Not so good.

How about this:

Austin Texas Mortgages by My Mortgage Co

That's pretty good. The keywords are front and center and the company name is right out there where everyone can see it. You could also put a separator of some kind instead of the word **by**. I think it's more of a personal preference than an important SEO point.

Each page of your web site needs its own page title. If your page titles repeat then several bad things might happen:

- You compete with yourself for ranking on your terms
- You confuse the search engine who thinks that you've got the same page twice
- You get hit with a duplicate content penalty
- You don't communicate well with your customers causing confusion

All these things can happen in Drupal if you're not careful. Luckily, there are a couple of modules that will really help with this.

Setting up your web site's name

The name of your web site will appear in many Page Titles throughout your site. Here's how you should set it:

1. Point your browser to `http://www.yourDrupalsite.com/admin/settings/site-information` or click **Site information** on the admin page.

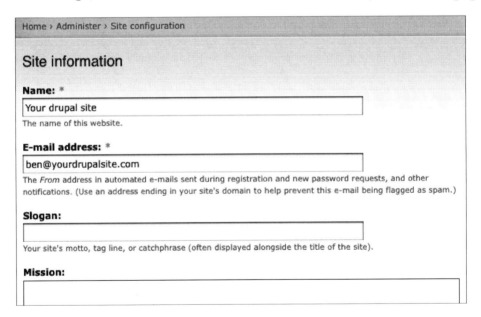

2. In the **Name** field, enter what you want your site to be called. This will appear wherever the name of your site is needed, including in many of your page titles, emails, and the header.
3. Finally, click on **Save configuration**.

Link titles

This section has talked a lot about page titles, but there is one other important title tag—**link title**. The link title is a bit of text that describes a link. It is used by the search engines to help determine what the linked-to page is about. It's also used in many browsers as a tool tip or hover text—that text that shows up when you hover over a link but don't click on it.

In plain HTML, a link title would appear as an element of the <a> tag, as follows:

```
<a href = "http://www.drupal.org/" title = "Drupal Open Source
CMS">Drupal</a>
```

If you embed links in your body content, you'll need to add this element yourself. Drupal, being the friendly CMS that it is, tries to help you when it can. In Drupal navigation, the title element is handled by the **Description** field of the **Edit Menu Item** screen.

How to edit the title element of your navigation links

Carry out the following steps to edit the title element of your navigation link:

1. Visit the link, `http://www.yourDrupalsite.com/admin/build/menu` or go to the **Menus** link on your admin screen.

2. Select the menu where the navigation link, which you want to edit, appears.

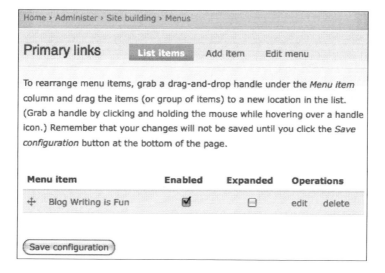

3. Enter the text that you want to appear as the link title in the **Description** field. Make sure that it has good keywords to indicate where the link is going. In this example, I wrote a blog post about writing fun blog posts. So, I want to use words like writing, blog, and fun.

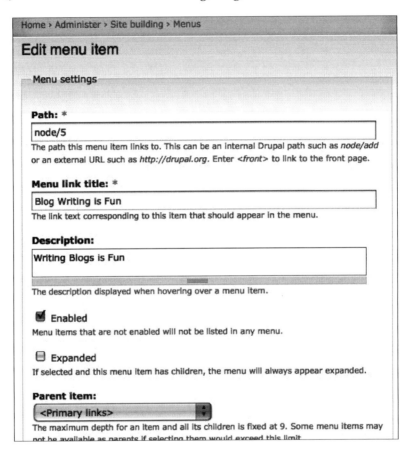

4. Click **Save**.

Make Drupal URLs clean and search engine optimized

As a web user, you know that the **URL** (**Universal Resource Locator**) is the address used by a browser to locate a certain piece of content. There's a lot of really cool tech with DNS and such that goes into making that happen that I'm not going to talk about here. What I will talk about is everything after the slash; in other words, `www.yourDruaplsite.com/everything-over-here`.

A brief history of static and dynamic URLs

The problem with database driven web sites (like any site built with Drupal) is that databases require a query that is not compatible with the URL system. A typical SQL database query requires spaces and strange, hieroglyphic-like symbols. Not pretty. So in the early days of web site building (way back in the mid-90s), clever developers came up with a method to pass database queries from a URL to the database, retrieve some data, and then pass it back to the visitor's browser. At the time this was revolutionary since most web sites were done in static HTML and were incredibly difficult to maintain, especially since most corporations store their data in huge databases.

The method they used involved a question mark (?), equal signs (=), and ampersands (&). It was magnificent until search engines came along. Search engines couldn't understand these often long, complex strings of data being passed from a browser to a server and back again. URLs often looked like this:

`www.reallyoldsite.com/?product=55697&lang=en&uid=bf663`

Yet, whenever you visit the following links you got the exact same content:

- `www.reallyoldsite.com/?product=55697&lang=en`
- `www.reallyoldsite.com/?product=55697`

As it turns out, the only important piece of this URL, at least as far as the search engines are concerned, was the first element. Even then, some sites would put the important things at the end of the URL and there was just no way for Google to know that. So, they ignored everything after the ?. That meant that web sites with thousands of products would look to Google like they only had one or two pages.

Therefore, the following web sites:

- `www.reallyoldsite.com/?product=55697`
- `www.reallyoldsite.com/?product=54861`
- `www.reallyoldsite.com/?product=99385`

Would all look as follows, to Google:

- `www.reallyoldsite.com`

Epic Fail!

Finally, in 1996, a really clever guy named Ralf Engelschall came up with a URL rewriting patch for Apache called **mod_rewrite**. It acts as a translator between URLs and databases, so that ugly query strings that confused search engines before now show up clean and friendly. You could now see the data that used to show up at the following link:

`www.reallyoldsite.com/?product=55697`

At this new URL:

`www.reallyoldsite.com/product/55697`

And all was right with the world.

How Drupal handles dynamic URLs

Just like the web sites of old, Drupal uses a query string to pull information from a database. Every blog post, comment, content, user entry, and so on is stored in tables on the server so you need a query string to go find the data and bring it back to the browser window. Here are some examples of standard Drupal URLs:

- `http://www.yourDrupalsite.com/?q=node/1`
- `http://www.yourDrupalsite.com/?q=taxonomy/term/7+19+20+21`
- `http://www.yourDrupalsite.com/?q=user/login`

> **Clean URLs** are URLs that do not contain any strange characters like ?, =, &, (,), or $. In Drupal, a clean URL looks like this: `http://www.yourDrupalsite.com/node/1`. Don't confuse a clean URL with a properly optimized one, though. While a clean URL can be easily read, it doesn't tell the search engines anything about your web site. **Search Engine Optimized URLs** actually contain some keywords. An example would be `http://www.yourDrupalsite.com/austin-real-estate`. This points to the same content; however, it has an indicator about that content. In this case, Austin real estate.

Turning on clean URLs in Drupal

During installation Drupal 6 will run the clean URL test automatically and will show the results. If you weren't the one to install Drupal or you don't remember whether it worked or not, you should check to make sure that clean URLs are turned on.

1. Point your browser to `http://www.yourDrupalsite.com/admin/settings/clean-urls` or go to your admin screen and click **Clean URLs**.

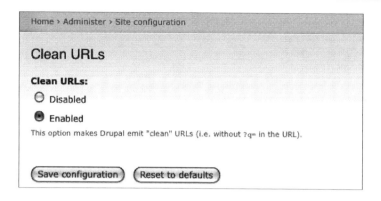

2. The **Enabled** radio button should be selected. If it is not, select it and click **Save configuration**.

If you cannot enable clean URLs

It's possible that your hosting company has some settings they need to adjust for you or that you need to edit your .htaccess file to make it work. Visit http://drupal.org/node/15365 for common configuration issues. There are solutions listed for clean URL problems with 1and1, Mac OS X, Bluehost, and GoDaddy.

Optimizing URLs with the Path module

Clean URLs are not enough. Sure, search engines can read the URL but that's just the first step to making your web site addresses work for you. Search engines look at the URL for keywords just like they look at the Page Title or the body content. That means that a site with keywords in the URL path will do better than a site without them. Thankfully, Drupal core includes the Path module which lets you write your own paths.

The **path** is the part of the URL that comes after the top level domain (com, org, edu, biz, info, and us are a few examples of the top level domains) but before any question marks (? indicates the beginning of the query strings that are passed to the database). For example, in the URL http://www.yourDrupalsite.com/node/2 the path is node/2.

The Path module allows you to manually create search engine friendly URLs based on your content. This allows you to get addresses that look like the following URLs:

- `http://www.yourDrupalsite.com/golf/best-american-courses.html`

instead of,

- `http://www.yourDrupalsite.com/node/8457`

or even

- `http://www.yourDrupalsite.com/?q=node/8457.`

The Path module was originally written and maintained by the great Matt Westgate, who has contributed early and often to Drupal's success. Thanks, Matt! As of Drupal 4.3, the Path module was rolled up into Drupal core.

How to turn on the Path module

Although the Path module is part of Drupal core, it's not turned on by default. To turn it on:

1. Visit the link, `http://www.yourDrupalsite.com/admin/build/modules` or go to the admin screen and click on **Modules**.

2. Find the **Core - optional** section and then find **Path**. Add a check in the box.

3. Click on **Save configuration**.

4. Now visit `http://www.yourDrupalsite.com/admin/user/permissions` or go to **Admin | User management | Permissions** and give permissions to users that need to create custom paths.

How to change a content path

1. Point your browser at the node for which you want to create a custom path.

   ○ To create new content, visit `http://www.yourDrupalsite.com/node/add`

   ○ To edit existing content, browse to that node and click on the **Edit** tab

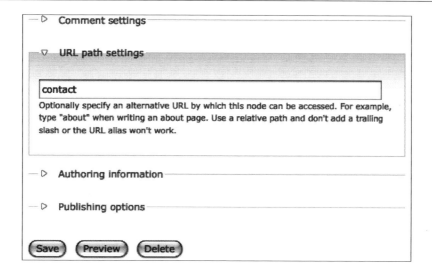

2. In the URL path settings field, put the path that you wish to show in the URL. Only put the text that shows up after the / that comes after the base URL. For example, if you want the alias to be `http://www.yourDrupalsite.com/contact` then you would put `contact` in the field. Do not put a trailing slash but you can put slashes in the field to simulate directories. For example, if you put `contact/austin-office` it would show up like this: `http://www.yourDrupalsite.com/contact/austin-office`.

3. Click on the **Save** button.

Writing optimized URLs

Writing optimized URLs is straightforward if you know your keywords. Simply put your keywords in the path separated by dashes.

*   `http://www.yourDrupalsite.com/gaming-computer`

It can be helpful to simulate hierarchy if you have a lot of content that goes together. You would do that like this:

*   `http://www.yourDrupalsite.com/computer/tower`
*   `http://www.yourDrupalsite.com/computer/tower/gaming/`
*   `http://www.yourDrupalsite.com/computer/tower/business/`

Use file extensions

It's a good idea to use file extensions on the pages you create for your web site. First, when Google visits your site, they're trying to figure out what kind of page they're looking at. They do a pretty good job of identifying HTML, PHP, XML, EXE and other type of files but you can help them out by including .html, .htm, or .php as a file extension. Second, many users pay attention to the links they're clicking on and telling them that they're going to land on a standard HTML page can be reassuring in this day and age of fishing and virus attacks. It can just add that little bit of reassurance they need to visit your page with confidence.

Automating paths with Pathauto and Path Redirect

One of the great things about Drupal is its ability to automate things that you've been doing manually up until now. With the PathAuto module, you can tell Drupal to automatically give a path to any new content you create based on a pattern that you define in the admin screens. Path Redirect gives some excellent SEO options that you should use when using PathAuto. We'll look at both.

PathAuto is co-maintained by Greg Knaddison, Mike Ryan, and Frederik "Freso" S. Olesen. Great job, guys!

Path Redirect is maintained by Dave Reid. Well done! (I'm a huge fan of Dave's — he does the new and improved XML Sitemap module too!)

Installing Pathauto and Path Redirect

You can download the Pathauto and Path Redirect modules from the following links:

- http://drupal.org/project/pathauto
- http://drupal.org/project/path_redirect

Both modules install as per normal Drupal modules. See Chapter 1, *The Tools You'll Need*, for step-by-step module installation instructions.

Be sure to turn on both modules on the **Modules** admin page: http://www.yourDrupalsite.com/admin/build/modules.

Configuring Pathauto

Carry out the following steps to configure Pathauto:

1. Visit the link `http://www.yourDrupalsite.com/admin/build/path/pathauto`, or click on **Administer | Site Building | URL Aliases | Automated alias settings**.

2. Open the **General Settings** drop-down. Your screen will look similar to the following screenshot:

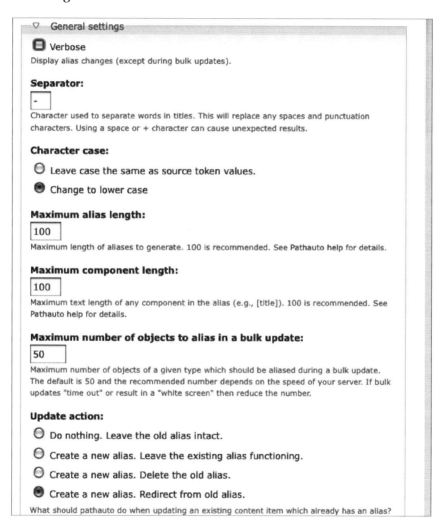

○ **Verbose**: This setting will give you a lot of information about what Pathauto is doing for you when you save a node. Typically, it is only used for testing your installation or configuration. It's a lot of fun but might be confusing for your users on a day-to-day basis.

○ Created new alias *blogs/admin/2009/feb/25/testing-2* for *node/4*, replacing *blogs/admin/2009/feb/3/testing-2*. *blogs/admin/2009/feb/3/testing-2* now redirects to *blogs/admin/2009/feb/25/testing-2*

○ Created new alias *blogs/admin/2009/feb/25/testing-2/feed* for *node/4/feed*, replacing *blogs/admin/2009/feb/3/testing-2/feed*. *blogs/admin/2009/feb /3/testing-2/feed* now redirects to *blogs/admin/2009/feb/25/testing-2/feed*

○ Blog entry *Testing for 2!* has been updated.

○ **Separator**: Set as -. This is the symbol that Pathauto will use instead of a space. Google says that _ is OK; however, - is preferred.

○ **Character case**: Set as Change to lower case. Set the **maximum alias length** to **100, maximum component length** to **100,** and the **maximum number of objects** to **alias** in a bulk update to 50. The update action will be as follows:

Create a new alias. Redirect from old alias: Recommended. This setting is great for new sites or old sites that you want to create a new structure for the content. If an old alias exists, it will create a new one and also create a 301 redirect from the old to the new location. This will preserve the PageRank and other values of the old page and pass them on to the new page. We'll cover 301 redirects in more detail later in this chapter.

Do nothing. Leave the old alias intact: This setting will leave any existing aliases as they are. If your site has been around for a while and has a lot of pages, then this might be a good option so that your content doesn't appear to be moving around.

Create a new alias. Leave the existing alias functioning: This will create two (or more) pages on your site with the exact same content. They're not actually two pages; just two different URLs that Drupal knows to show the same data. This confuses search engines and you should avoid duplicate content where possible.

Create a new alias. Delete the old alias: This will delete any old locations in your site which will create broken links in Google. Google doesn't like broken links. Plus any incoming links from other web sites will not resolve and you'll end up losing all your rankings. Not a good idea. The only time this is OK is if you are renaming all your links and you didn't have much ranking in Google anyway. Still, a redirect is probably a safer bet.

○ **Transliterate prior to creating alias**: If your site is international or your users may create content with accents or other non-US characters, this tool will change all those characters into their **ASCII-96** equivalent. This is easier for search engines that primarily display data in English to index and display. If you use this option, you will need to have an i18n-ascii.txt file in the Pathauto directory. You can see an example file here: `http://drupal.org/files/issues/ i18n-ascii.example.txt`

ASCII-96 is a standard set of characters based on the English alphabet. They are: !"#$%&'()*+,-./0123456789:;<=>?@

ABCDEFGHIJKLMNOPQRSTUVWXYZ [\]^_`

abcdefghijklmnopqrstuvwxyz{|}~

Reduce strings to letters and numbers from ASCII-96: Filters the new alias to only letters and numbers found in the ASCII-96 set. This will delete any non ASCII-96 characters.

Strings to remove: This will strip out a list of common words from the URL, that is, a, an, as, at, but, the, and so on. This helps with SEO because those common words don't communicate to the search engines what your site is about.

Default strings to remove: a, an, as, at, before, but, by, for, from, is, in, into, like, of, off, on, onto, per, since, than, the, this, that, to, up, via, with

Consider adding these: it, you, that, he, was, for, are, i, his, they, be, one, have, or, had

○ **Punctuation settings**: Defines what to do with any punctuation that is translated by the PathAuto filter. In general, you can leave the default settings.

◦ **Blog Path settings**: This setting is only for the location of each main blog page. You'll set the location of each individual blog post in the next section.

Pattern for blog page paths: This is the first place that you get to decide what you want the PathAuto filter to do. You can use Tokens (PathAuto calls them **Replacement patterns**) to tell it to rename the blogs on your web site using data available in the database. The default is **blogs/[user-raw]**. However, you may want to call your blogs journals. You might put **journals/[user-raw]**. Leave the field blank and it will not do any automatic replacements at all.

Bulk generates aliases for blogs that are not aliased: This setting is just what it sounds like: If there are any blogs on your site that do not have aliases, Pathauto will create one.

Internal feed alias text (leave blank to disable): The text to use for aliases for RSS feeds. Examples are **feed** and **0/feed**. PathAuto is not just for nodes, it will alias your RSS feeds, too. Use this field to set the pattern for your feed URLs.

◦ **Node path settings**: The real power of PathAuto, this section is for naming the paths of all your node types. Any node type that you create or turn on should be listed here.

Default path pattern (applies to all node types with blank patterns below): This is the default. If you plan on having the same path for all node types then this is the only field you need.

Pattern for paths: Enter how you want each node path to be displayed.

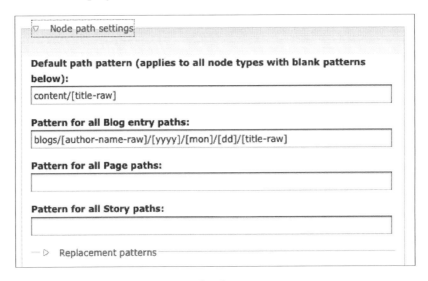

Path Goal:	Try This:	To show this URL
by Date	blogs/[author-name-raw]/[yyyy]/[mon]/[dd]/[title-raw]	`yourDrupalsite.com/blogs/ben/2010/Feb/22/my-36th-birthday`
by Category	[vocab-raw]/[term-raw]/[title-raw]	`yourDrupalsite.com/categories/personal/my-36th-birthday`
by Menu	[menupath-raw]/[menu-link-title-raw]	`yourDrupalsite.com//my-36th-birthday`
by Keyword	keyword/[title-raw]	`keyword/my-36th-birthday`

> **Bulk generate aliases for nodes that are not aliased**: Check this if you want to use these settings to generate aliases for all existing nodes which do not already have aliases. Good for creating a lot of aliases at once. But, be sure you've tested your settings on a couple of nodes first to make sure you'll get the results you want.

> **Internal feed alias text (leave blank to disable)**: The text to use for aliases for RSS feeds. Examples are **feed** and **0/feed**. PathAuto is not just for nodes, it will alias your RSS feeds too. Use this field to set the pattern for your feed URLs.

- ○ **Taxonomy term path settings**: This section is for naming the paths of all your taxonomy terms. It works just like the other sections except that the replacement patterns are geared toward taxonomies like the vocabulary name.

- ○ **User path settings**: This section allows you to specify the path for each user account. User paths can contain things like the date they registered and the username. If you're building a social networking site, pay special attention to this section.

Redirects

Changing of URLs causes the following problems:

- People who bookmarked the page can't find it again
- Search engines can't find your content
- People who link to your pages now have broken links

The best advice, then, is to never change your URLs. The practicality, however, is that there are many reasons that a URL might need to be changed:

- Companies acquire web sites and need to move content
- Products become obsolete so the content needs to move to a different section of the site
- Keywords change so content that was relevant before doesn't fit

Redirects came into being because webmasters need a way to tell visitors and search engines that content has moved from point A to point B on the server. In its most basic form, a redirect simply tells a browser to go to a different page. For example, you want people who visit www.yourDrupalsite.com/expensive-cars/Ferrari to automatically move on to www.yourDrupalsite.com/cars/expensive/Ferrari. This helps to maintain a clean site that doesn't break when content gets moved around.

301 Redirects—the right way to move content around

Two years ago, you might have created a path that looked like this:

```
http://www.yourDrupalsite.com/expensive-cars/Ferrari
```

But now, you realize that it would be better to have a path looking like this:

```
http://www.yourDrupalsite.com/cars/expensive/Ferrari
```

In Drupal, this is easy. The actual content sits at a node reference location; for example, node/123. So you just have to create a new alias, right? Not so fast! Although it is possible to assign multiple aliases to a node, this is probably not a good idea from an SEO perspective. If Google sees two identical pages on your web site, they're not going to know which one is the most important. In the best case, your pages will actually compete with each other in Google for the top spot. In the worst, Google might think you're trying to spam your way to the top and penalize your site.

However, if you simply delete the old URL then you have a situation where someone who may have bookmarked the old location will now get a **404 – Page Not Found** error. Even worse, if you've spent some time getting links to that old page, a 404 error is a sure way of discouraging people to link to you in the future. Finally, a missing page is like telling Google that you're closed for business and so send those users somewhere else. That's not the message you want to send.

To prevent this situation, you need something called a **301 redirect or a Permanent Redirect**. It tells visitors (including the search engines) that this content is permanently moved to the new location. For search engines, a permanent redirect means a few different things, as follows:

- They'll show the new URL in the search listings instead of the old one.
- They'll eventually stop sending their crawler around to that old URL.
- Most importantly, they'll give credit for any links pointing the old URL to the new URL. So, all that hard work you did to build links carries over. Nice!

Note that these things may take some time—probably about two weeks for Google, longer for MSN and Yahoo.

Installing and configuring Path Redirect

The Path Redirect module is great for getting your site redirects working properly. Carry out the following steps to install and configure Path Redirect:

1. Download the Path Redirect module from the link `http://drupal.org/ project/path_redirect` and install it just like a normal Drupal module. Refer to Chapter 1 for step-by-step module installation instructions.

2. Visit `http://www.yourDrupalsite.com/admin/build/path-redirect/ settings` or click on **Admin | Site Building | URL Redirects | Settings**.

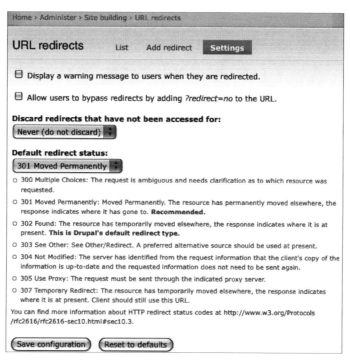

3. Perform the following actions under the **Settings** option:

   ○ **Display a warning message to users when they are redirected**: Set to not ticked. This will avoid displaying a warning message like the following:

   Page not found

   This page has been moved to http://www.yourdrupalsite.com/blogs/admin/2009/feb/25/testing-2. You will be automatically redirected in 10 seconds.

   The requested page could not be found.

   ○ **Allow users to bypass redirects by adding '?redirect=no' to the URL:** Set to not ticked. Although, unlikely, if you have this setting turned on then you could create duplicate content if someone links to the `?redirect=no` link. It's great for testing but not worth the risk on production sites.

   ○ **Discard redirects that have not been accessed for:** Set to **Never** (do not discard). This will make sure that any old URLs are still redirected. If you run a huge site and are worried about database bloat, you could set this to 1 Year or even less. However, this is not an appreciable performance issue for most sites.

   ○ **Default redirect status**: Set to **301 Moved Permanently.** This tells search engines that the content is gone and not coming back. There are other options but this is the best one most of the time.

4. Click on **Save configuration.**

How to set up a 301 redirect

Carry out the following steps to set up a 301 redirect:

1. Make sure you have the Path Redirect module installed. It installs like any other Drupal module.

2. Set up the new alias for your content. Go to `http://www.yourDrupalsite.com/admin/build/path/add` or from the admin screen click on **Site Building | URL Aliases | Add Alias**.

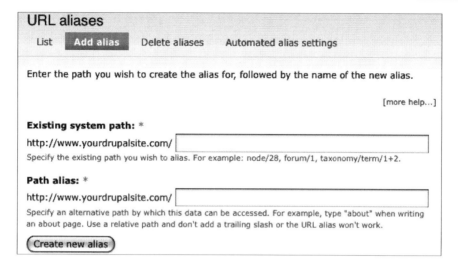

URL aliases

List   **Add alias**   Delete aliases   Automated alias settings

Enter the path you wish to create the alias for, followed by the name of the new alias.

[more help...]

Existing system path: *

http://www.yourdrupalsite.com/ [   ]

Specify the existing path you wish to alias. For example: node/28, forum/1, taxonomy/term/1+2.

Path alias: *

http://www.yourdrupalsite.com/ [   ]

Specify an alternative path by which this data can be accessed. For example, type "about" when writing an about page. Use a relative path and don't add a trailing slash or the URL alias won't work.

(Create new alias)

3. Under the **Existing system path** option, put the **real** location for the content. For example, **node/128**, **forum/12**, and so on.

> The **real** URL of the content can be hard to find. The easy way is to click the **Edit** link at the top of the content. You'll find the URL to be something like `http://www.yourDrupalsite.com/node/5/edit`. Just take off the `/edit`. So, the real URL for this content is `http://www.yourDrupalsite.com/node/5`.

4. Under the **Path alias** option, put the text you would like to use as the alias, like **cars/expensive/Ferrari**. do not add a slash before or after the text in this field.

5. Click on **Create new alias**.

> Don't stop here! Be sure to complete steps 6-8 to finish creating your 301 redirect or you will have duplicate content on your site and risk penalties from the search engines.

6. Now, that you've created the alias, let's redirect the old alias to the new one. Go to `http://www.yourDrupalsite.com/admin/build/path-redirect/ add` or click on **Administer | Site Building | URL Redirects | Add redirect**.

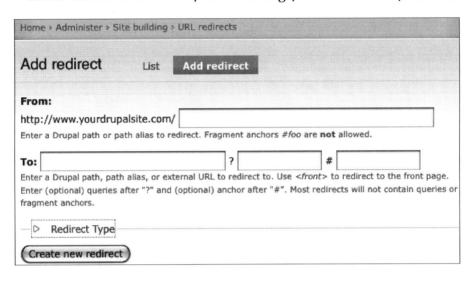

-   Under the **From** option, enter the old path. For example, `http://www.yourDrupalsite.com/ expensive-cars/Ferrari`.

-   Under the **To** option, enter the new path. For example, `http://www.yourDrupalsite.com/cars/ expensive/Ferrari`.

-   Under the **Redirect Type** option, make sure **301 Moved Permanently** is selected. The other kinds of redirects are very rarely used. In general, you always want to use a 301 unless you know what you're doing. To find out more, visit the following link, `http://www.w3.org/Protocols/rfc2616/ rfc2616-sec10.html#sec10.3`.

7. Click **Create new redirect**.

8. Test the new alias to make sure that it works the way you want it to.

Alternate way to create 301s

The Path Auto module will automatically create 301s for you when you rename the path in the node edit screen. Just make sure that you have Path Auto configured to **Create a new alias. Redirect from old alias.**

How long should I keep redirects?

How long you keep redirects depends on a couple of things. For the search engines index, I would only keep them for a couple of months. However, if someone has bookmarked that page or put a link to it on their web site, maybe you should keep it longer. I would keep them as long as there are still people using them. You can do this very easily by telling the Path Redirect module to automatically delete redirects after a certain period of disuse. I like sixteen weeks or a year. That means that one year after its last use, the redirect will be deleted.

Global Redirect module—fixing Drupal's duplicate content problems

The Global Redirect module takes care of some housekeeping issues that come up when clean URLs are enabled in Drupal. Let's say, for example, that you create a new web site and create the first node that you call **My First Post**. Later, because you want the front page of your site to be the content of that node, you go into site settings and make node/1 the front page of the site. Sounds pretty harmless, right? Well, right at this moment, all of these URLs on your site would show the exact same content:

- http://www.yourDrupalsite.com/
- http://www.yourDrupalsite.com/?q=node/1
- http://www.yourDrupalsite.com/node/1
- http://www.yourDrupalsite.com/node/1/
- http://www.yourDrupalsite.com/my-first-post
- http://www.yourDrupalsite.com/my-first-post/

So, the search engines will think that you have six pages of the exact same content. That's not good. Global Redirect fixes that by redirecting all the URLs you don't want to the one URL that you do. Here's the logic that Global Redirect uses (sourced from http://drupal.org/project/globalredirect):

1. Checks the current URL for an alias and does a 301 redirect to it if it is not being used.

2. Checks the current URL for a trailing slash, removes it if present, and repeats check 1 with the new request.

3. Checks if the current URL is the same as the site_frontpage and redirects to the frontpage if there is a match.

4. Checks if the Clean URLs feature is enabled and then checks the current URL is being accessed using the clean method rather than the **unclean** method.

5. Checks access to the URL. If the user does not have access to the path, then no redirects are done. This helps avoid exposing private aliased nodes.

6. Make sure the case of the URL being accessed is the same as the one set by the author/administrator. For example, if you set the alias "articles/cake-making" to node/123, then the user can access the alias with any combination of case.

That's a lot of work for one module and it does it quite well. Thanks for this module, Nicholas Thompson! By the way, Nick and I did a podcast together a while back about the Global Redirect module. Listen in here: `http://www.volacci.com/podcast/episode3`.

Canonical Links

In February 2009, a new setting came out from Google, Yahoo, and MSN (Live) called the canonical link. Canonical means "this is the best choice of all the duplicate content on my web site". It's a new link tag in the header of a web page designed to fix this problem of duplicate content on web sites. A webmaster indicates which duplicate page is the right one and that's the one that the search engines will index. However, in a video explaining canonical links on Google, (`http://www.google.com/support/webmasters/bin/answer.py?answer=139394`) Google's search engine spam prevention guru, Matt Cutts, says that the best thing to do is to fix your CMS. Thanks to the Global Redirect module (and if you have your other modules configured properly), Drupal doesn't need canonical links.

How to install and configure the Global Redirect module

Carry out the following steps to install and configure the Global Redirect module:

1. The Global Redirect module installs just like any other Drupal module. Refer to Chapter 1, *The Tools You'll Need*, for step-by-step module installation instructions.

2. To configure the module, point your browser to `http://www.yourDrupalsite.com/admin/settings/globalredirect` or click on **Admin | Site configuration | Global Redirect**. You should see something like this:

Home › Administer › Site configuration

Global Redirect

Deslash:

○ Off

● On

If enabled, this option will remove the trailing slash from requests. This stops requests such as `example.com/node/1/` failing to match the corresponding alias and can cause duplicate content. On the other hand, if you require certain requests to have a trailing slash, this feature can cause problems so may need to be disabled.

Non-clean to Clean:

○ Off

● On

If enabled, this option will redirect from non-clean to clean URL (if Clean URL's are enabled). This will stop, for example, node 1 existing on both `example.com/node/1` AND `example.com?q=node/1`.

Remove Trailing Zero Argument:

● Disabled

○ Enabled for taxonomy term pages only

○ Enabled for all pages

If enabled, any instance of "/0" will be trimmed from the right of the URL. This stops duplicate pages such as "taxonomy/term/1" and "taxonomy/term/1/0" where 0 is the default depth. There is an option of limiting this feature to taxonomy term pages ONLY or allowing it to effect any page. **By default this**

3. The default settings are the right ones for most web sites. However, it can be helpful to know what's going on with Global Redirect (Source: Global Redirect help text).

   ° **Deslash**: Set to **On**. If enabled, this option will remove the trailing slash from requests. This stops requests such as `yourDrupalsite.com/node/1/` failing to match `yourDrupalsite.com/node/1` and creating duplicate content. On the other hand, if you require certain requests to have a trailing slash, this feature can cause problems and so may need to be disabled.

   ° **Non-clean to Clean**: Set to **On**. If enabled, this option will redirect from Non-clean to Clean URL (if Clean URL's are enabled). This will stop, for example, node 1 existing on both `yourDrupalsite.com/node/1` and `yourDrupalsite.com?q=node/1`.

      °   **Remove Trailing Zero Argument**: Set to **Disabled**. If enabled, any instance of /0 will be trimmed from the right of the URL. This stops duplicate pages such as taxonomy/term/1 and taxonomy/term/1/0 where 0 is the default depth. There is an option of limiting this feature to taxonomy term pages only or allowing it to affect any page. By default this feature is disabled to avoid any unexpected behavior.

      °   **Menu Access Checking**: Set to **Disabled**. If enabled, the module will check the user has access to the page before redirecting. This helps to stop redirection on protected pages and avoids giving away secret URL's. By default this feature is disabled to avoid any unexpected behavior.

      °   **Case Sensitive URL Checking**: Set to **Enabled**. If enabled, the module will compare the current URL to the alias stored in the system. If there are any differences in case then the user will be redirected to the correct URL.

4.   Click **Save configuration**.

Now your site is protected from duplicate content. Great job!

Summary

In this chapter, we covered the most important aspects of on-page SEO for your Drupal site: Page Titles and Paths. We have covered the following aspects:

- Page Titles—what they are, how to write good ones, and how to configure them on Drupal site
- Link Titles
- Clean URLs
- Optimizing URL paths with the Path, Path Auto, and Path Redirect modules
- Redirects—what they are, how to set them up in Drupal, and how the Path Redirect and Global Redirect modules help you avoid deadly duplicate content on your web site

We've done a lot; however, there's still plenty more left to do if you want to make your site as optimized as it could be. In the next chapter, we continue to rock the Drupal SEO house with more on-page optimization.

4

More On-Page Optimization

So, by now, you're making great progress on your site. You've done your page titles and renamed your site, your navigation has great titles, your URLs are clean and SEO-optimized, and those paths are keyword rich and built to stay that way. On top of that, you've redirected all your old content using 301s and installed the Global Redirect module to address duplicate content issues. Whew! You're doing great but there's a bit more to do. This chapter will continue with the on-page optimization that your site needs:

- Headings
- Drupal Menus and Navigation
- Optimizing images, video, and other media
- Meta Tags with the Meta Tags module

Ready? Let's do it!

Headings

HTML, and its follow-ons, allow for a special kind of text called **Headings**. Headings are different than page titles in that they are visible while page titles are not. Headings normally show up large and bold at the top of a web site. These are terrific indicators of what the page is about and should be integral to the site structure. Unfortunately, they're easy to abuse. Generally speaking, you should only have one H1 tag on each page of your web site. However, many site owners put H1 tags around anything that they want bolded, bigger, or search engine-optimized. This is a mistake and it's confusing to readers and to Google.

What if you were standing in a bookstore and opened a book called **My Life in Kenya**. You flip over to Chapter 1 and see the title, Chapter 1: *I like Kenya*, but later down the page you see big, bold font that says 'How to Succeed in Business' and a page or two later you see 'How to Play Baseball'. You would have no idea what that book is really about and, chances are, you'd drop it back on the shelf and head over to the coffee counter for a stiff double latte to clear your head. Unfortunately, many Drupal site owners are doing the exact same thing with their H1 tags.

More than one H1 is fine, but only if...

Matt Cutts, the director of Google's search spam prevention team, released a video in early 2009 that said that having 2 or 3 `<H1>` tags per page is OK if they're truly defining sections of the page that should be set off as different ideas or concepts. `http://budurl.com/mch1`. It's not OK to just use them willy-nilly whenever you want to bold something; use `<strong>` or `<emphasis>` to set apart ideas in the text of your site. Use H2, H3, and so on to set apart subsections or major ideas that appear on the same page.

HTML Header tags

As an identifier, the `<H1>` tag on your web site works just like a chapter title in a book. The text between `<H1>` and `</H1>` should communicate exactly what that one page is all about. If there is further information or subsections on the page, you can use `<H2>`, `<H3>`, all the way up to `<H6>` heading tags to show hierarchical organization on the page. While it is OK to have multiple `<H2>` to `<H6>` tags, be sure to only use a single `<H1>` on any one page of your web site.

Imagine that you're writing an outline. So, each `<H2>` tag should be a subtopic of the `<H1>` tag. Don't use a **hanging** heading tag, either. Only use an `<H6>` if you have an `<H5>` above it, do not use an `<H5>` unless you have an `<H4>` above it, and so on. Make sure the body text in each section is relevant to the headings above it.

Each page has its own headings. The headings from your front page don't carry over to any other page. Ideally, each page of your site has a different heading that accurately reflects its own unique content to your users and the search engines.

How Drupal handles headings

The default Drupal theme—Garland—doesn't handle H1 tags particularly well. In fact, it assumes that the most important thing on every single page of your web site is the site name. While it may be important for the front page to have the H1 as the site name (or maybe not, more on that a bit later), it is certainly not the most important thing on every single page of your site. On the deeper pages, the most important thing on the page will vary. It could be a category, a product, a service, the name of your CEO, or whatever that page is about.

Other themes are even worse. I won't name them outright but some themes (Pushbutton) put <H1> tags around the entire node titles on the front page. That's a disaster. It's like saying that this page is about, well, everything. I'm not saying not to use those themes. They're actually nice, usable, and compatible themes. Just be sure you pay attention and fix any SEO-related problems with the theme that you choose.

Ideally, here's how you want to do your heading tags in Drupal:

- **Front page of your site**: <H1> should be around the most important keywords that you want to rank for your front page. If you list nodes on your front page, put <H2> tags around each node title.

- **Single Node view**: <H1> should be around the most important keywords that you want to rank for that particular page. Use <H2> around any subsection headings of that page—this is likely done in the node body.

- **Lists** (nodes, users, taxonomies, and so on): <H1> should be around the most important keywords that describe that list. (For example, if it's a category page on an e-commerce site, what are the keywords that describe that category?). Put <H2> around the titles in the list.

In Drupal, the best way to build <H1> tags into your site is to put them into the theme. Be sparing though! Too many headings make a page hard to read and difficult for the search engines to determine what it's all about. This book is not a theming book but it's straightforward to accomplish this in your Drupal theme.

 For more information about how to set up your theme, visit the following link, http://drupal.org/theme-guide/6.

Drupal menus and navigation

The menu—or even just a list of links to take visitors around in your site—can make a big difference to your site's indexability and standing in the search engines. In Chapter 3, *On-Page Optimization*, we discussed how to make title attributes for your navigation links. Now, let's take it to the next level and make sure that the keywords in your site's internal navigation give insight into the subject of the site. The anchor text of your own navigation is one of the places that Google looks to determine what your site is about.

How to change your navigation

First, think about your navigation. Where are you sending people when they click? What does it mean when you have a **Home** link in your navigation? If you're not selling real estate, chances are that **Home** is not a good choice to bring people back to the front page of your site. Figure out what your customers call your products or services—not what your industry calls them—and then make your navigation accordingly. Once you know what you want to call each navigation item, carry out the following steps:

1. Point your browser to `http://www.yourDrupalsite.com/admin/build/menu` or go to your admin screen and click the **Menus** link. You'll see something like this:

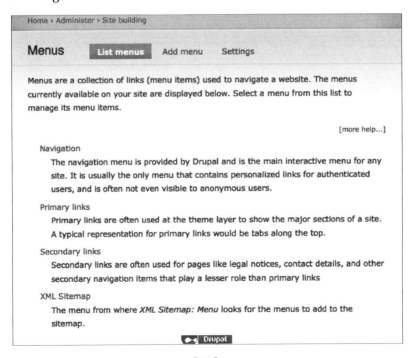

2. Now click the link to the menu where you've placed your site's navigation items. You will see a list of all the menu items on your site.

3. Click the **Edit** link next to each item that you wish to change. You will see a screen similar to the following screenshot:

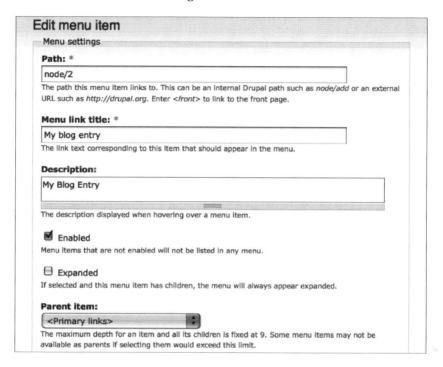

4. Type the search engine optimized text into the **Menu link title** field. For example, if you own a sports car dealership, you might put **Fast Cars** here.

5. Click on the **Save** button.

Other links in your site

Your site navigation is not the only place that may contain links to your site. Putting links in the body of your text to other relevant pages of your site is a great way to guide visitors through your site. Here are a few best practices for links:

- Don't use CSS to make links look like plain text. Make them look like links. If it doesn't clash with your theme, use blue text with underlining since everyone is already familiar with that style.

- Use helpful, keyword-rich anchor text for the links. Avoid **Click Here** or **Here** as the anchor text. It tells Google nothing about where the link is going. Instead, use words that indicate what the user will find if they click the link like this: `<a href = "/category/fastpc.php">Fast PCs.</a>`

- Don't put more than about 100 links on a page. It's overwhelming to users and looks like spam to Google.

Optimize images, video, and other media

Images are everywhere on the web. Video, Flash, and other media are not far behind. Great graphics, animations, or videos add a lot of value to an otherwise boring web site. The drawback is that search engine spiders cannot read the content of these files. Nothing kills your site's searchability faster than embedding all your best keywords into graphic or Flash files. Users see them just fine but search engines see nothing. It is extremely important to communicate as much information as you can to the search engines about each graphic or media piece that you use on your site.

Google Image Search uses the file name and the alt tag to determine what the image is all about. Other services, like YouTube, Viddler, and video search engines, need help to determine what your video is about so that they can show it to people that are interested in watching your masterpiece. Make sure that you can take advantage of these powerful streams of traffic by adhering to the following guidelines.

 Did you know that, as of mid-2009, Google-owned YouTube is 2nd ranked search engine in the world? It's behind Google's main search engine but ahead of such industry stalwarts as Yahoo and Bing. With that kind of power, you can't afford to ignore the power of video on your web site.

File name

The first and easiest way to identify what the file is about is to use a descriptive file name. A filename like `img0004.jpg` does nothing for you. However, `president-obama-eats-donut.jpg` is descriptive, keyword-filled and does wonders for the findability of, say, a presidential pastries web site. The file extension (`.jpg`) also tells the search engines a lot about what that file is and how to display it to users. Make sure your videos have video extensions, your flash files have flash extensions, and so on.

Problem: Drupal's image upload feature renames the files into meaningless drivel.

Solution: Download the **FileField Paths** module from the following link, `http://drupal.org/project/filefield_paths`. This handy tool lets you use node tokens to rename images on upload. So, for example, you could use the node title as the source of the filename. This isn't perfect for every situation but it's a huge step in the right direction.

The alt and title attributes

The **alt** attribute specifies alternative text to display if the image, movie, or other media can't be displayed. Suppose someone has images turned off in their browser settings (common on dial-up connections and text-based browsers) or the images get moved. The alt text would be displayed instead. For search engines, the alt text can be another indicator of what that element of the page is about and thence, what the entire page or site is about.

Don't overdo alt and title tags!

Unfortunately, many **black-hat SEOs** have used alt and title text as a way to **stuff** keywords into their sites. This was a useful tactic...back in 1995. Just use alt and title tags as you would if you didn't care about SEO. Put keywords in there if it helps your users. Search engines are smart. They'll figure out if you're stuffing your keywords and penalize you in the search results.

Unlike the **page title**, the **title** attribute can be used to annotate many different things on a web site. Titles can be used on images, objects, applets, and more. (For more information, visit `http://www.w3.org/TR/REC-html40/struct/global.html#title`). Browsers display the title text in different ways. It is what will be displayed when a mouse hovers over that object or what will be read if your visitors are using screen reading software.

Uses of alt and title

Many web designers want to use graphics instead of text to represent links or menu options. While this may be helpful to users, text links are better for SEO and are preferred by search engines because they can't read graphics. If you do decide to use a graphic as a link, be sure to include the title attribute as Google will view the title text for that image a lot like the anchor text of a text link. Make sure the title text for graphical links describe the page where the link it pointed, not the page that it is on.

In addition, use the alt element in the graphic itself to reinforce the meaning to the search engines. For example, your graphical navigation links should look something like this:

```
<a href = "/training-videos" title = "Training Videos"><img src = "/
files/training-video-thumb.jpg alt = "Training Videos"></a>
```

In Drupal 6, to effectively control the alt and title attributes of media files requires the **Content Construction Kit**, commonly known as **CCK**. The Content Construction Kit allows you to add custom fields to nodes using a web browser. If you're not using it already you will be soon, as much (but not all) of the functionality of CCK is moving into Drupal 7 core.

Want to become a CCK ninja?

Check out the awesome Learning CCK for Drupal video from Lullabot: http://store.lullabot.com/. In this tutorial video, Drupal heavyweights Jeff Eaton, Nate Haug, and James Walker show everything from CCK basics such as adding and displaying fields to more advanced topics such as CCK's database storage mechanisms, field-level permissions, and how to theme CCK's output.

To take full control of the media, including alt and titles, you'll need the following modules:

- CCK: http://www.drupal.org/project/cck
- FileField module: http://drupal.org/project/filefield
- ImageField module: http://drupal.org/project/imagefield
- ImageField tokens: http://drupal.org/project/imagefield_tokens

Text near the media file

Another great way to optimize a media file for Google consumption is to make sure that the text nearest to the file is relevant to that file and contains your keywords. It's important to remember that text that looks close to an image on the screen may actually be somewhere else on the site. If you're concerned, look at the source code of the site to determine if the text is in the right place. Use a good description of what the visitor is seeing and put your best keywords first in that paragraph.

One great way to generate a lot of good text for video files is to create a word-for-word text transcript. Put the transcript on the site right next to the video. Easy.

Meta tags

Meta tags are pieces of text in the header of your web site that tell search engine spiders about your site. They are not visible to your site visitors, which make them handy places to communicate details about your site that visitors just don't care about. The problem is that in the stone age of search engines (1997) many people abused the meta tags by stuffing them full of keywords. This was invisible to their visitors but the search engines gave a lot of credence to the meta tags, so it was a viable way to get to the top of the search engines. Nowadays, most search engines ignore meta tags as a ranking mechanism but do take them into account for other things, so they're important to maintain on your sites.

There are about a dozen different meta tags that you can use but here are the main ones that you should care about.

Meta type	Description	What it looks like
Copyright	States the copyright of the site.	`<meta name="copyright" content="© Copyright 2010 Yourcorp, Inc. All rights reserved." />`
Description	A two- or three-sentence description of the content of the page. Used by many search engines in the search results as the text under your link.	`<meta name="description" content="Your Description" />`
Keywords	A list of six to eight relevant keywords for this page. Largely abused so it's ignored by Google and most other engines.	`<meta name="keywords" content="your, keywords,here" />`
Geo Position	Attributes a specific geographical location to your site. It helps search engines, like Google, who display different results based on the location of the searcher.	`<meta name="geo.position" content="30.4363439; -97.7728595" />`

Meta type	Description	What it looks like
ICBM	This is another geo tag. Yes, it really does mean the address needed to drop a nuke on your head. More geeky humor from the people who make the Internet.	`<meta name="ICBM" content="30.4363439, -97.7728595" />`
Robots	Used if you cannot control the `robots.txt` file on your site. This would be useful if content creators want to request that search engines not index their pages on your site.	`<meta name="robots" content="index,follow" />`

Metadata is a fancy word that is used in the information sciences to mean **data about this data**. Saying meta data is easier than saying data data; however, that's basically what it means. So, you could say that this section is data about metadata. Or, meta metadata. Does that mean that this information box is meta meta meta data? OK, I'll stop now.

In Drupal, it's very easy to set meta tags for each node thanks to the Meta tags module. This handy module gives you some extra fields on each node that you create so that you can put in a description, keywords, and other meta data as you want. It's even integrated with the Tokens module to provide you with plenty of automatic data population.

This incredibly useful module is maintained by Robrecht Jacques and Alberto Paderno. Thank you and grazie!

Installing the Meta tags module

Carry out the following steps to install the Meta tags module:

1. Download the Meta tags module from the following link:
    `http://drupal.org/project/nodewords`

2. Install as per normal Drupal modules. See Chapter 1, *The Tools You'll Need*, for step-by-step module installation instructions.

3. Be sure to turn on the module on the Modules admin page:
    `http://www.yourDrupalsite.com/admin/build/modules`.

☑	**Meta tags**	6.x-1.0	Allows users to add meta tags, eg keywords or description.

4. Adjust the permissions, as needed, at the following link:
   `http://www.yourDrupalsite.com/admin/user/permissions`.

Is it the Meta tags module or the Nodewords module?

They're one and the same, actually. The early versions of the module were designed to add keywords to nodes, hence node keywords or Nodewords. But, over time the module has grown to include more than just the keywords meta tag so the name needed updating. Now, the preferred name is Meta tags. The old name keeps hanging around, though, because making a name change to a Drupal module is a lot like nailing Jello to a wall—it just doesn't stick. Call it what you will, we should all be thankful for the Meta node keyword tags module.

Configuring the Meta tags module

Carry out the following steps to configure the Meta tags module:

1. Go to `http://www.yourDrupalsite.com/admin/content/nodewords` or click on **Administer | Content Management | Meta tags.** You'll see something like this:

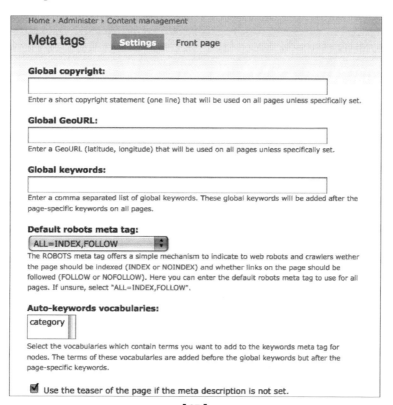

2. The Global copyright, Global GeoURL, Global keywords, and Default robots meta tag are the site-wide defaults. If you don't specifically set these elements in the node, then the Meta tags module will display the ones that you set here. Here are some examples of what you might put into these fields:

   ° Global copyright: © Copyright 2010 Yourcorp Corporation. All rights reserved
   ° Global GeoURL: 30.4363439, -97.7728595
     (Note: despite what is showing in the help notes below this field, do not put parenthesis around your latitude and longitude)
   ° Global keywords: computers, servers, gaming pcs
   ° Default robots meta tag: `ALL=INDEX, FOLLOW`

3. The Auto-keywords vocabularies field allows you to select the taxonomy categories that you would like to include in the keywords field. Here's how it works:

   ° Select any taxonomy on the Meta tags configuration page.
   ° When you create a node, include terms from the taxonomy that you selected.
   ° When you save the node, the terms that you selected will now be included in the keywords Meta tag. You can verify this by looking at the source of the page in your browser.

4. Further down the configuration page, you'll see this:

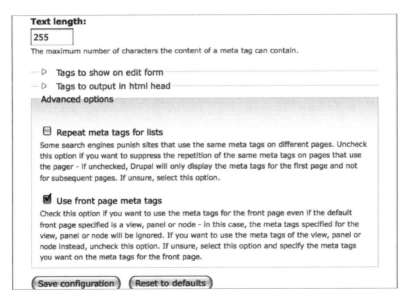

5. You'll probably want to leave these configuration settings as the defaults, but let's review them:

   ○ **Text length**: Defines the maximum length of a meta tag. Most search engines won't look beyond 255 characters.

   ○ **Tags to show on edit form**: Specify which meta tags you want you or your content creators to be able to edit on a node-by-node basis. For most, description and keywords are all you should allow. However, if you want users to be able to opt content out of Google, give them control over the Robots meta tag. GeoURL would allow users to define their pages in a different geographical location than the rest of the site.

   ○ **Tags to output in html head**: You can turn on or off any meta tags that you want or don't want to appear on your site. For example, if you're not a geographically focused business, you might turn off the GeoURL meta tag.

   ○ **Repeat meta tags for lists**: As you build up content on your site, you'll notice that some pages, like the home page and taxonomy pages, will use pagination. That means that they'll show the ten most recent nodes and then offer links to subsequent ones. This option allows you to specify if you want meta tags to show up on the paginated pages of a long list of content. If you uncheck this option, you'll have meta tags on the first page of paginated content only. Check it and meta tags will show up on all pages. Most sites should leave this option unchecked.

   ○ **Use front page meta tags:** The Meta tags module allows you to specify meta tags for the front page of the site. In Drupal, there are many ways to define the front page. You can make it a node, a list of nodes, a view, a panel, and more. You could even specify different front pages based on the role of the currently logged-in user. With this option, you have an opportunity to define the meta tags no matter how the front page of the site may be defined. Most sites should check this box and then...

6. Define the front page meta tags by visiting the following link, `http://www.yourDrupalsite.com/admin/content/nodewords/frontpage` or clicking on **Administer | Content Management | Meta tags | Front page**. You'll see a screen similar to the following screenshot:

- ○ **Description**: Enter the description of the front page of the site. This is usually a two or three-sentence description of the content of the page that is used by many search engines in the search results as the text under your link. It's very important because it's what a search engine user will see before they click on your link.

- ○ **Keywords**: Enter a comma-separated list of keywords about your site.

7. Click on **Save**.

Specifying meta tags for your content

Now that you have the Meta tags module installed and properly configured, you can start specifying meta tags for all the content that you create.

Taxonomy meta tags

Since taxonomy is a very broad kind of content on your web site, it is a great idea to use broad, category-like keywords on this page.

Taxonomy is how to classify something in Drupal. Many sites' first taxonomy is **category**. Taxonomy can have subsections (subcategories) called **terms**. Terms can have subterms, and so on. In Drupal, it's very easy to see all the content that is in a certain category by visiting the taxonomy list for that term. Let's say you've created a taxonomy called **products** and a term called **computers**. The URL for the taxonomy list should be something like this: `http://www.yourDrupalsite.com/category/products/computers`.

1. Go to `http://www.yourDrupalsite.com/admin/content/taxonomy` or click on **Administer | Content Management | Taxonomy**.

2. If you would like to edit an existing vocabulary, click **edit vocabulary** next to the one you'd like to edit. To create a new one, click **Add vocabulary**. You should see a screen similar to the following screenshot:

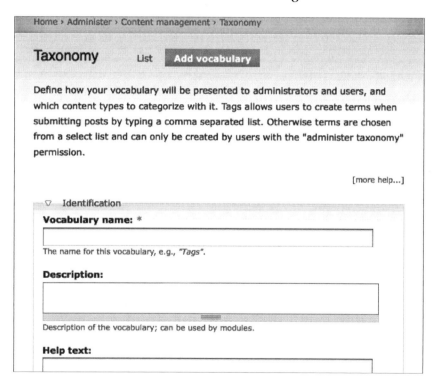

3. Enter in the details you want. Further down, you'll notice some new fields:

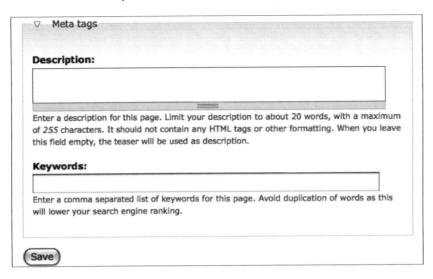

4. Enter the description in the **Description** field and the keywords in the **Keywords** field, which you want for this taxonomy.

5. Click on **Save**.

You can do this for each taxonomy term too. Since terms are a more specific kind of content on your web site, use specific categories for the keywords on this page.

1. Go to `http://www.yourDrupalsite.com/admin/content/taxonomy` or click on **Administer | Content Management | Taxonomy**.

2. Next to the taxonomies, click on **List**. You'll see a list of your terms as shown in the following screenshot:

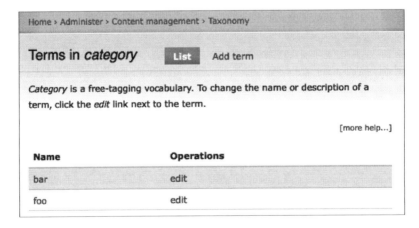

3. Click on the **edit** link. You'll see the meta tags fields listed near the bottom of the edit screen.

4. Enter your meta tags into the fields provided.

5. Click on **Save**.

Node meta tags

The basic form of content in your Drupal site is a node. Every node is a page of its own but can also be used in other ways, like a list or a block. The Meta tags that you specify for a node will only be displayed when that node, and that node alone, is on the page.

Since a node is the most specific kind of content on your web site, it is a great idea to use very specific, long-tail keywords on this page.

1. To edit an existing node, navigate to that node and click the **Edit** link. To create a new node, go to http://www.yourDrupalsite.com/node/add or navigate to **Administer | Content management | Create Content** and select the type of node you'd like to create.

> ### Create content
>
> Blog entry
> A *blog entry* is a single post to an online journal, or *blog*.
>
> Page
> A *page*, similar in form to a *story*, is a simple method for creating and displaying information that rarely changes, such as an "About us" section of a website. By default, a *page* entry does not allow visitor comments and is not featured on the site's initial home page.
>
> Story
> A *story*, similar in form to a *page*, is ideal for creating and displaying content that informs or engages website visitors. Press releases, site announcements, and informal blog-like entries may all be created with a *story* entry. By default, a *story* entry is automatically featured on the site's initial home page, and provides the ability to post comments.

2. You'll see the Meta tags fields listed near the bottom of the edit screen.

3. Enter your Meta tags into the fields provided.

4. Click on **Save**.

Views meta tags

Views is the single most commonly installed module in Drupal. So, it's important enough to cover Meta tags for Views here.

1. Meta tags can only be added to existing Views. If the View that you need doesn't exist yet, create it and then edit it.

2. To edit an existing View, visit the following link, `http://www.yourDrupalsite.com/admin/build/views/list`, or navigate to **Administer | Site building | Views** and click on the **Edit** link next to the View that you wish to edit. You should see a screen similar to the following screenshot:

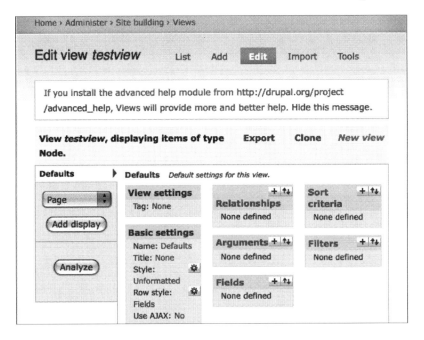

3. You'll see the meta tags fields listed near the bottom of the edit screen.

4. Enter your meta tags into the fields provided.

5. Click on **Save**.

Summary

In this chapter, we have covered more of the all-important aspects of on-page SEO for your Drupal site. We covered the following points:

- Headings — what they are, how to use them for SEO, and how to set them up in Drupal
- Drupal menus and navigation — leveraging them for SEO purposes
- Optimizing images, video, and other media
- Meta tags with the Meta tags module

Now that you've got your site all nice and Search Engine Optimized, it's time to tell the world! In the next chapter, we're going to explore the fastest way to get the entire content of your web site uploaded to Google and the other search engines — sitemaps.

5
Sitemaps

As smart as the Google spider is, it's possible for them to miss pages on your site. Maybe you've got an orphaned page that isn't in your navigation anymore. Or, perhaps you have moved a link to a piece of content so that it's not easily accessible. It's also possible that your site is so big that Google just can't crawl it all without completely pulling all your server's resources — not pretty!

The solution is a **sitemap**. There are three different kinds of sitemaps that we're going to cover in this chapter, each with a different purpose:

- **XML sitemaps** are designed to be easily used by search engines
- **URL-list sitemaps** simply list every URL in your site
- **Visitor-facing sitemaps** create a nice interface for your site visitors to help them easily find the content on your site that they're looking for

In this chapter, we shall cover:

- What sitemaps are and why you should use them
- How to install sitemaps on your Drupal site
- How to submit the XML sitemaps to Google
- Other things you can do once they're installed

Let's get started.

XML sitemaps

In the early 2000s, Google started supporting **XML sitemaps**. Soon after Yahoo came out with their own standard and other search engines started to follow suit. Fortunately, in 2006, Google, Yahoo, Microsoft, and a handful of smaller players all got together and decided to support the same sitemap specification. That made it much easier for site owners to make sure every page of their web site is crawled and added to the search engine index. They published their specification at `http://sitemaps.org`. Shortly thereafter, the Drupal community stepped up and created a module called (surprise!) the XML sitemap module. This module automatically generates an XML sitemap containing every node and taxonomy on your Drupal site. Actually, it was written by Matthew Loar as part of the Google Summer of Code. The Drupal 6 version of the module was developed by Kiam LaLuno. Finally, in mid-2009, Dave Reid began working on a version 2.0 of the module to address performance, scalability, and reliability issues. Thanks, guys!

According to `www.sitemaps.org`:

> *Sitemaps are an easy way for Webmasters to inform search engines about pages on their sites that are available for crawling. In its simplest form, a Sitemap is an XML file that lists URLs for a site along with additional metadata about each URL (when it was last updated, how often it usually changes, and how important it is, relative to other URLs in the site) so that search engines can more intelligently crawl the site.*

> *Web crawlers usually discover pages from links within the site and from other sites. Sitemaps supplement this data to allow crawlers that support Sitemaps to pick up all URLs in the Sitemap and learn about those URLs using the associated metadata.*

Using a sitemap does not guarantee that every page will be included in the search engines. Rather, it helps the search engine crawlers find more of your pages. In my experience, submitting an XML Sitemap to Google will greatly increase the number of pages when you do a **site:** search.

The keyword **site:** searches show you how many pages of your site are included in the search engine index, as shown in the following screenshot:

Setting up the XML Sitemap module

The XML Sitemap module creates a sitemap that conforms to the `sitemap.org` specification.

Which XML Sitemap module should you use?

There are two versions of the XML Sitemap module for Drupal 6. The 1.x version is, as of this writing, considered the stable release and should be used for production sites. However, if you have a site with more than about 2000 nodes, you should probably consider using the 2.x version. From `www.drupal.org`: 'The 6.x-2.x branch is a complete refactoring with considerations for performance, scalability, and reliability. Once the 6.x-2.x branch is tested and upgradeable, the 6.x-1.x branch will no longer be supported'. What this means is that in the next few months (quite possibly by the time you're reading this) everyone should be using the 2.x version of this module. That's the beauty of open source software—there are always improvements coming that make your Drupal site better Search Engine Optimized.

The rest of this chapter refers to XML Sitemap module version 2.x Beta.

Carry out the following steps to set up the XML Sitemap module:

1. Download the XML Sitemap module from the following link,
   `http://drupal.org/project/xmlsitemap` and install it just like a normal
   Drupal module. See Chapter 1, *The Tools You'll Need*, for step-by-step
   module installation instructions. When you go to turn on the module,
   you'll be presented with a list that looks similar to the following screenshot:

▽ XML sitemap			
Enabled	**Name**	**Version**	**Description**
☐	**XML sitemap**	6.x-2.x-dev	Creates an XML sitemap conforming to the sitemaps.org protocol. Required by: XML sitemap custom (disabled), XML sitemap engines (disabled), XML sitemap menu (disabled), XML sitemap node (disabled), XML sitemap taxonomy (disabled)
☐	**XML sitemap custom**	6.x-2.x-dev	Adds user configurable links to the sitemap. Depends on: XML sitemap (disabled)
☐	**XML sitemap engines**	6.x-2.x-dev	Submit the sitemap to search engines. Depends on: XML sitemap (disabled)
☐	**XML sitemap menu**	6.x-2.x-dev	Adds menu item links to the sitemap. Depends on: XML sitemap (disabled), Menu (enabled)
☐	**XML sitemap node**	6.x-2.x-dev	Adds content links to the sitemap. Depends on: XML sitemap (disabled)
☐	**XML sitemap taxonomy**	6.x-2.x-dev	Add taxonomy term links to the sitemap. Depends on: XML sitemap (disabled), Taxonomy (enabled)

Before you turn on any included modules, consider what pieces of content
on your site you want to show up in the search engines and only turn on the
modules you need.

- The **XML sitemap** module is required. Turn it on.
- **XML sitemap custom** allows you to add your own
  customized links to the sitemap. Turn it on.

- ° **XML sitemap engines** will automatically submit your sitemap to the search engines each time it changes. This is not necessary and there are better ways to submit your sitemap (like the robots.txt file which we'll cover in the next chapter). However, it does a nice job of helping you verify your site with each search engine. Turn it on.
- ° **XML sitemap menu** adds your menu items to the sitemap. This is probably a good idea. Turn it on.
- ° **XML sitemap node** adds all your nodes. That's usually the bulk of your content so this is a must-have. Turn it on.
- ° **XML sitemap taxonomy** adds all your taxonomy term pages to the sitemap. Generally a good idea but some might not want this listed. Term pages are good category pages so I recommend it. Turn it on.
- ° Don't forget to click **Save configuration**.

2. Go to `http://www.yourDrupalsite.com/admin/settings/xmlsitemap` or go to your admin screen and click on **Administer | Site Configuration | XML sitemap** link. You'll be able to see the **XML sitemap**, as shown in the following screenshot:

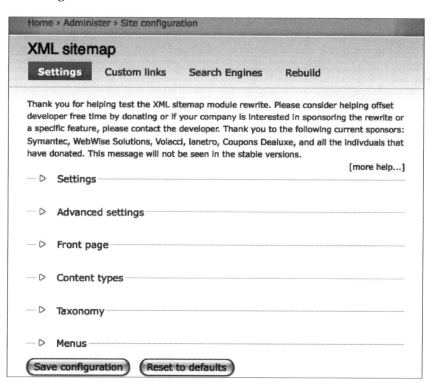

3. Click on **Settings** and you'll see a few options, as shown in the following screenshot:

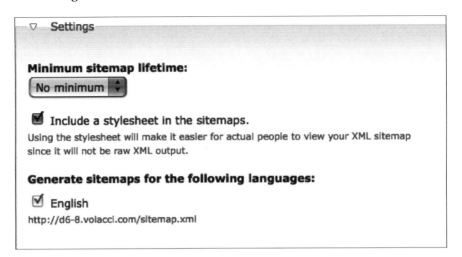

- ○ **Minimum sitemap lifetime**: It determines that minimum amount of time that the module will wait before renewing the sitemap. Use this feature if you have an enormous sitemap that is taking too many server resources. Most sites should leave this set on **No minimum**.

- ○ **Include a stylesheet in the**: The **sitemaps** will generate a simple css file to include with the sitemap that is generated. It's not necessary for the search engines but very helpful for troubleshooting or if any humans are going to view the sitemap. Leave it checked.

- ○ **Generate sitemaps for the following languages**: In the future, this option will allow you to actually specify sitemaps for different languages. This is very important for international sites who want to show up in localized search engines. For now, **English** is the only option and should remain checked.

4. Click the **Advanced settings** drop-down and you'll see several additional options.

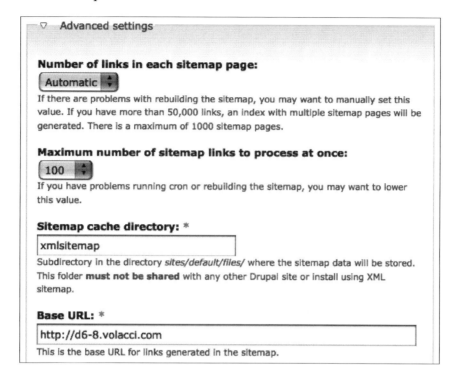

- ○ **Number of links in each sitemap page** allows you to specify how many links to pages on your web site will be in each sitemap. Leave it on **Automatic** unless you are having trouble with the search engines accepting the sitemap.

From www.sitemaps.org:

'You can provide multiple Sitemap files, but each Sitemap file that you provide must have no more than 50,000 URLs and must be no larger than 10MB (10,485,760 bytes). If you want to list more than 50,000 URLs, you must create multiple Sitemap files. If you do provide multiple Sitemaps, you should then list each Sitemap file in a Sitemap index file.'

- ○ **Maximum number of sitemap links to process at once** sets the number of additional links that the module will add to your sitemap each time the cron runs. This highlights one of the biggest differences between the new XML sitemap and the old one. The new sitemap only processes new nodes and updates the existing sitemap instead of reprocessing every time the sitemap is accessed. Leave this setting alone unless you notice that cron is timing out.

  - ○ **Sitemap cache directory** allows you to set where the sitemap data will be stored. This is data that is not shown to the search engines or users; it's only used by the module.

  - ○ **Base URL** is the base URL of your site and generally should be left as it is.

5. Click on the Front page drop-down and set these options:

  - ○ **Front page priority**: 1.0 is the highest setting you can give a page in the XML sitemap. On most web sites, the front page is the single most important part of your site so, this setting should probably be left at 1.0.

  - ○ **Front page change frequency**: Tells the search engines how often they should revisit your front page. Adjust this setting to reflect how often the front page of your site changes.

What is priority and how does it work?

Priority is an often-misunderstood part of a sitemap. For instance, the priority is only used to compare pages of your own site and you cannot increase your ranking in the **Search Engine Results Page (SERPS)** by increasing the priority of your pages. However, it does help let the search engines know which pages of your site you feel are more important. They could use this information to select between two different pages on your site when deciding which page to show to a search engine user.

6. Open the **Content types** drop-down and you will see the following screenshot:

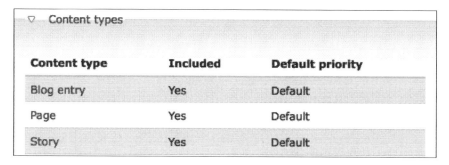

- ° Here, you will see each **Content type** listed separately. You probably want to leave these settings alone so that all your content shows up in the sitemap.

- ° If you do want to adjust the **Content types** settings in the sitemap, you'll need to go to the content type screen. Click on the name of the content type to go to that screen.

- ° On the content type screen, open the **XML sitemap** drop-down and you'll see two options.

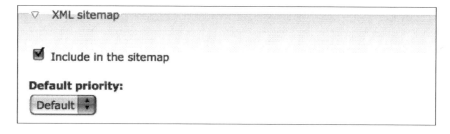

- ○ **Include in sitemap** sets the default action for that content type – if you check this box then it will be included in the sitemap.

- ○ **Default priority** allows you to set the default for each node that you create of that content type. Default is usually .5 but you can adjust it if you want certain pages of a higher or lower priority.

- ○ Click on **Save content** type.

- ○ Repeat for each content type that you wish to change.

7. Click **Save configuration**.

8. Now, you need to run **cron**. Cron is a recurring script that takes care of many maintenance issues in Drupal including populating the XML sitemap. To run cron, point your browser to `http://www.yourDrupalsite.com/cron.php` and wait until the page stops loading. You will not receive any indication that it's complete except that your browser will stop loading the page.

9. Point your browser to `http://www.yourDrupalsite.com/sitemap.xml`. If you see a bunch of gobbledygook that looks like the following screenshot:

Or a screen similar to the following screenshot:

Sitemap file: http://www.yourdrupalsite.com/sitemap.xml

Number of URLs in this sitemap: 76

Click on the table headers to change sorting.

URL location	Last modification date	Change frequency	Priority
http://www.yourdrupalsite.com/		daily	1.0
http://www.yourdrupalsite.com/content/enim	2009-08-10T15:45:21+00:00	hourly	0.5
http://www.yourdrupalsite.com/content/si-consequat-qui-vulpes-luptatum	2009-08-10T15:45:23+00:00	daily	0.5
http://www.yourdrupalsite.com/content/inhibeo-genitus	2009-08-10T15:45:23+00:00	monthly	0.5
http://www.yourdrupalsite.com/content/qui-acsi-obruo-secundum-meus	2009-08-10T15:45:24+00:00	monthly	0.5
http://www.yourdrupalsite.com/content/macto-interdico	2009-08-10T15:45:25+00:00	weekly	0.5
http://www.yourdrupalsite.com/content/tation-quis-ratis-jus	2009-08-10T15:45:25+00:00	daily	0.5
http://www.yourdrupalsite.com/content/quadrum-quadrum-dolor-lucidus-vero	2009-08-10T15:45:25+00:00	weekly	0.5
http://www.yourdrupalsite.com/content/loquor-enim-sed-quidne-sudo-metuo	2009-08-10T15:45:25+00:00	weekly	0.5
http://www.yourdrupalsite.com/content/ullamcorper	2009-08-10T15:45:26+00:00	weekly	0.5
http://www.yourdrupalsite.com/content/ulciscor	2009-08-10T15:45:26+00:00	weekly	0.5
http://www.yourdrupalsite.com/content/comis-quadrum-incassum-minim-praemitto	2009-08-10T15:45:27+00:00	daily	0.5
http://www.yourdrupalsite.com/content/esse-defui-hendrerit-abdo-refoveo-fere	2009-08-10T15:45:21+00:00	monthly	0.5

10. If yes, then you've done it right! If you view the source code of the sitemap, you'll see something like the following screenshot:

```
<?xml version="1.0" encoding="UTF-8"?>
<?xml-stylesheet type="text/xsl" href="/sitemap.xsl"?>
<urlset xmlns="http://www.sitemaps.org/schemas/sitemap/0.9">
<url><loc>http://www.yourdrupalsite.com/</loc><changefreq>daily</changefreq>
<priority>1.0</priority></url>
<url><loc>http://www.yourdrupalsite.com/content/enim</loc>
<lastmod>2009-08-10T15:45:21+00:00</lastmod><changefreq>hourly</changefreq></url>
<url><loc>http://www.yourdrupalsite.com/content/si-consequat-qui-vulpes-luptatum</loc>
<lastmod>2009-08-10T15:45:23+00:00</lastmod><changefreq>daily</changefreq></url>
<url><loc>http://www.yourdrupalsite.com/content/inhibeo-genitus</loc>
<lastmod>2009-08-10T15:45:23+00:00</lastmod><changefreq>monthly</changefreq></url>
<url><loc>http://www.yourdrupalsite.com/content/qui-acsi-obruo-secundum-meus</loc>
<lastmod>2009-08-10T15:45:24+00:00</lastmod><changefreq>monthly</changefreq></url>
<url><loc>http://www.yourdrupalsite.com/content/macto-interdico</loc>
<lastmod>2009-08-10T15:45:25+00:00</lastmod><changefreq>weekly</changefreq></url>
<url><loc>http://www.yourdrupalsite.com/content/tation-quis-ratis-jus</loc>
<lastmod>2009-08-10T15:45:25+00:00</lastmod><changefreq>daily</changefreq></url>
<url><loc>http://www.yourdrupalsite.com/content/quadrum-quadrum-dolor-lucidus-vero</loc>
<lastmod>2009-08-10T15:45:25+00:00</lastmod><changefreq>weekly</changefreq></url>
<url><loc>http://www.yourdrupalsite.com/content/loquor-enim-sed-quidne-sudo-metuo</loc>
<lastmod>2009-08-10T15:45:25+00:00</lastmod><changefreq>weekly</changefreq></url>
<url><loc>http://www.yourdrupalsite.com/content/ullamcorper</loc>
<lastmod>2009-08-10T15:45:26+00:00</lastmod><changefreq>weekly</changefreq></url>
<url><loc>http://www.yourdrupalsite.com/content/ulciscor</loc>
<lastmod>2009-08-10T15:45:26+00:00</lastmod><changefreq>weekly</changefreq></url>
<url><loc>http://www.yourdrupalsite.com/content/comis-quadrum-incassum-minim-praemitto</loc>
<lastmod>2009-08-10T15:45:27+00:00</lastmod><changefreq>daily</changefreq></url>
<url><loc>http://www.yourdrupalsite.com/content/esse-defui-hendrerit-abdo-refoveo-fere</loc>
<lastmod>2009-08-10T15:45:21+00:00</lastmod><changefreq>monthly</changefreq></url>
<url><loc>http://www.yourdrupalsite.com/content/torqueo-et-jumentum-dolor</loc>
<lastmod>2009-08-10T15:45:27+00:00</lastmod><changefreq>daily</changefreq></url>
<url><loc>http://www.yourdrupalsite.com/content/tum-scisco-singularis-exerci</loc>
<lastmod>2009-08-10T15:45:27+00:00</lastmod><changefreq>weekly</changefreq></url>
<url><loc>http://www.yourdrupalsite.com/content/premo</loc>
<lastmod>2009-08-10T15:45:28+00:00</lastmod><changefreq>weekly</changefreq></url>
<url><loc>http://www.yourdrupalsite.com/content/immitto-patria-nunc</loc>
<lastmod>2009-08-10T15:45:28+00:00</lastmod><changefreq>weekly</changefreq></url>
<url><loc>http://www.yourdrupalsite.com/content/quis-fere-nunc-ad-eum</loc>
```

The XML Sitemap will only update when cron runs. On a normal Drupal installation, you should have set cron to run periodically – nightly for most sites or more often for high-traffic sites.

Specifying the XML sitemap priority for nodes

Now that you have the XML sitemap module properly installed and configured, you can start defining the priority of the content on your site – by default, the priority is .5. However, there are times when you may want Google to visit some content more often and other times when you may not want your content in the sitemap at all (like the comment or contact us submission forms).

Each node now has an XML sitemap section that looks like the following screenshot:

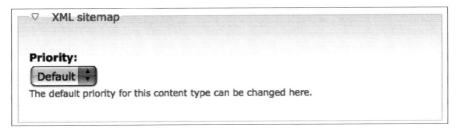

You can adjust the priority on a node-by-node basis by changing the default. You can even omit nodes from the sitemap by selecting **Not in site map**.

Submitting your XML sitemap to Google

Carry out the following steps in order to submit your XML sitemap to Google:

1. If you have not already done so, you need to verify your web site with Google Webmaster Tools. Refer to Chapter 1, *The Tools You'll Need*, for details.

2. Now point your browser to Google's Webmaster Tools at `http://www.google.com/Webmasters/`. Click on **Sign in to Webmaster Tools**, as shown in the following screenshot:

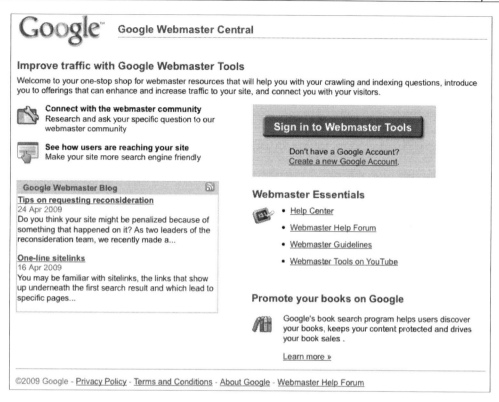

3. You should see a list of your sites. Click on the **Add** link in the **Sitemap** column, located to the right of your site link, as shown in the following screenshot:

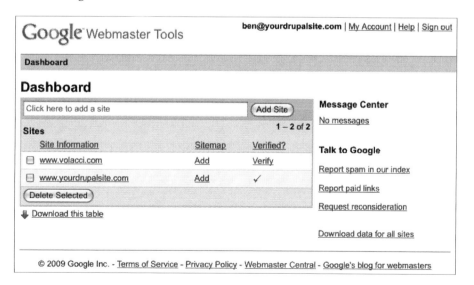

4. Double-check that your sitemap is working.

5. Copy and paste your sitemap URL (`http://www.yourDrupalsite.com/sitemap.xml`) into the blank space provided and click on **Submit Sitemap**. NOTE: If you get an error in Google, try tweaking your URL by adding `?q=` after the /, as follows:

`http://www.yourDrupalsite.com/?q=sitemap.xml)`

6. You should see a confirmation message that looks like this:

7. Now wait for several hours…or days.

8. Log in to Google Webmaster Tools, click your domain and then click the **Sitemaps | Overview**. If the status is still **Pending** then wait a bit longer. When your sitemap has been crawled, it will say **OK**.

>
> **Track who sees the XML sitemap**
>
> You can easily see who has accessed your XML Sitemap by visiting your Watchdog log: `http://www.yourDrupalsite.com/admin/reports/dblog`. You can see how recently each search engine has visited your sitemap.

What about all those other search engines out there? It's easy to let them all know where your XML Sitemap is located by adding it to your `robots.txt` file. We'll cover that in the robots.txt section in Chapter 7, *robots.txt, .htaccess, and W3C Validation.*

Google News XML Sitemap

Google has created one of the most popular news sources on the Internet just by collecting and organizing news articles from other sites. It's called **Google News** and if you are running a news web site then you know how powerful it can be for picking up your comment. One front page article can generate 50,000 or more visitors in an hour or two. To be listed in Google News takes more than luck. You need to write great content and proactively seek to create timely and news-worthy content. If you've done that and you're still not showing up in Google news then it's time to create a **Google News XML Sitemap**. The Google News sitemap generator module was originally created by Adam Boyse at Webopius and is being maintained by Dave Reid. Thanks to both of you!

Setting up the Google News sitemap generator module

1. Download the Google News sitemap module from `http://drupal.org/project/googlenews` and install it just like a normal Drupal module. See Chapter 1, *The Tools You'll Need*, for step-by-step module installation instructions.

2. Go to `http://www.yourDrupalsite.com/admin/settings/googlenews` or go to your admin screen and click the **Administer | Site Configuration | Google News sitemap feed** link. You'll see a screen similar to the following screenshot:

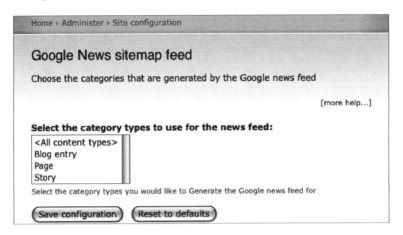

3. Select the content types that you wish to show up in the news feed. If all your story content types are newsworthy, pick **Story**. Your blog or page content types are probably not a good fit and selecting them may hurt the chances of your content being approved by Google.

4. Click on **Save configuration**.

5. Point your browser to `http://www.yourDrupalsite.com/googlenews.xml` and double check that you can see the sitemap, as shown in the following screenshot:

```
<!-- generator="googlenewsmodule/v1.0" -->
- <!--
    sitemap-generator-url="http://www.webopius.com" sitemap-generator-version="1.0"
  -->
- <urlset>
  - <url>
      <loc>http://www.yourdrupalsite.com/node-26-story</loc>
    - <news:news>
        <news:publication_date>2009-04-24T12:08:38-05:00</news:publication_date>
      </news:news>
  </url>
  - <url>
      <loc>http://www.yourdrupalsite.com/node-10-story</loc>
    - <news:news>
        <news:publication_date>2009-04-23T07:09:52-05:00</news:publication_date>
      </news:news>
  </url>
</urlset>
```

Submitting your Google News sitemap to Google News

Once you've assembled your new articles for a single publication label, submit them to Google News sitemaps by carrying out the following steps:

1. Check Google News to see if your site is already included. If not, you can request inclusion by visiting the following link, `http://www.google.com/support/news_pub/bin/request.py?ctx=answer`. The inclusion process may take up to a few weeks, and you'll only be able to submit a News sitemap once this process is complete.

2. If your site is already showing up in Google News then proceed. If not, you should wait a couple of weeks and try again.

3. Log in to Google Webmaster Tools by pointing your browser to `http://www.google.com/webmasters/tools/`.

4. On the **Webmaster Tools Dashboard**, click on **Add** next to the site you want to submit.

5. From the **Choose type** drop-down menu, select **News sitemap**, and then type the sitemap URL, in this case `http://www.yourDrupalsite.com/googlenews.xml`.

6. In the list, select the publication label for the articles. You can select only one label for each sitemap.

7. Click on **OK**.

URL list

The XML Sitemap is the ideal choice because it allows you to specify a lot of information about the content of your site. But, say for some reason that you can't install an XML Sitemap. Maybe there's a conflict with another module that you just have to have. Perhaps your server doesn't have the power to handle the large overhead that an XML sitemap needs for large sites. Or, possibly you want to submit a sitemap to a search engine that doesn't support XML yet.

Well, there is an alternative. It's not as robust but it is a functional, albeit rudimentary, solution. Just make a list of every URL in your site and put the list in one big text document with one URL on each line. Too much work, you say? Good thing there is a Drupal module that does all the work for you. It's called the **URL list** module. It's maintained by David K. Norman. Thank you, David!

Setting up a URL list sitemap

1. Download the Sitemap module from `http://drupal.org/project/urllist` and install it just like a normal Drupal module. See Chapter 1, *The Tools You'll Need*, for step-by-step module installation instructions.

2. Go to `http://www.yourDrupalsite.com/admin/settings/urllist` or go to your admin screen and click the **Administer | Site Configuration | URL list** link. You'll see the **URL list** screen, as shown in the following screenshot:

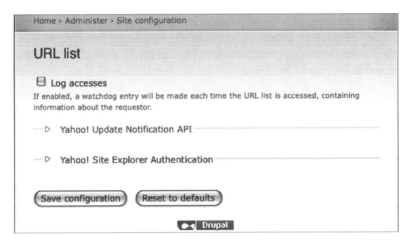

3. You can adjust the settings to keep track of who accessed the URL list to submit your site to Yahoo! and to help you authenticate with Yahoo!. However, you can leave all these settings untouched for now.

4. Point your browser to `http://www.yourDrupalsite.com/urllist.txt` (`http://www.yourDrupalsite.com/?q=urllist.txt` if you don't have clean URLs installed) and you'll see your URL list sitemap, as shown in the following screenshot:

You can submit this sitemap to Google, Yahoo!, and many other search engines in lieu of an XML sitemap. Just follow the same steps as defined in the Submit your XML Sitemap to Google section above but use `http://www.yourDrupalsite.com/urllist.txt` as the URL.

Remember to use `http://www.yourDrupalsite.com/?q=urllist.txt` if Google has problems with your URL.

Visitor-facing sitemaps

XML Sitemaps are great for search engines but as you can see, they're not user-friendly at all. Some of your site visitors will want to see all of the pages or sections available to them on your web site. That's where a **Visitor-facing sitemap** comes in handy. Fortunately, there is a Drupal module that will do that for you automatically! It's called the Site map module. Not only does it show you a nice overview of your site but it can show the RSS feeds too. Everybody raise a glass to Nic Ivy and Fredrik Jonsson, respectively the original author and current maintainer of this module. Cheers, gentlemen!

Setting up a visitor-facing sitemap

Carry out the following steps to set up a visitor-facing sitemap:

1. Download the Sitemap module from `http://drupal.org/project/site_map` and install it just like a normal Drupal module. See Chapter 1, *The Tools You'll Need*, for step-by-step module installation instructions.

2. Go to `http://www.yourDrupalsite.com/admin/settings/sitemap` or go to your admin screen and click the **Administer | Site configuration | Site Map** link. You'll see the Site map, as shown on the following screenshot:

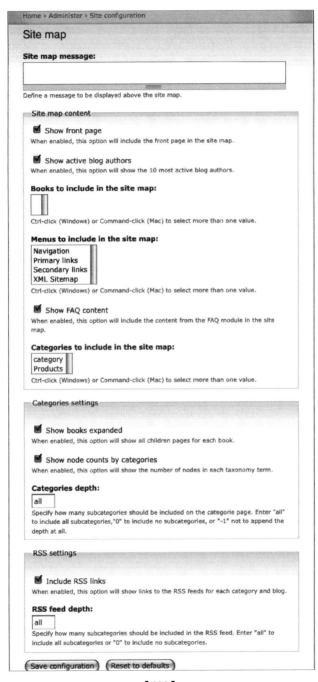

3. In the **Site map message** box, put a nice message that describes your site map. This is a great place to put a couple of keywords that generally describe your site.

4. The **Site map content** option will consist of the following:

    °   **Show front page**: This option allows you to decide whether or not to display the front page of your site in the sitemap. It's a personal preference and doesn't have much affect on your SEO.

    °   **Show active blog authors**: Shows or hides the ten most active blogs. Should be turned on for most sites that have blogs. If you don't have any blogs on your site, turn this option off.

    °   **Books to include in the site map**: If you're using the Book module then you can include your book sections in your sitemap. If you do have some books on your Drupal site then you should select them.

    °   **Menus to include in the site map**: Gives you control over which menus you should include in your sitemap. Be sure that only menus that you want visitors to see are selected here as you don't want to expose links to your admin or other non-visitor sections of your site. You probably should not turn on the **Navigation** menu.

    °   **Show FAQ content**: If you're using the FAQ module, this will show the content of your FAQ. Turn it on.

    °   **Categories to include in the site map**: This will allow you to show taxonomy terms in your sitemap. A great idea for most sites.

5. **Categories settings**: It's a good idea to turn on as much content in the sitemap as possible. However, try to find a balance between lots of good links into your site for your visitors and overwhelming them with too much information. Keep in mind that this sitemap is primarily for visitors, not search engines.

   ○ **Show books expanded**: Shows all the sections and child pages of your book.

   ○ **Show node counts by categories**: This shows a number next to each taxonomy term showing how many items are in that term. This can be helpful information to your visitors.

   ○ **Categories depth**: Specify the number of subcategories that should be included under each category. Enter **all** to include all subcategories, **0** for no subcategories, or **-1** to not append the depth of each category. This can be confusing at first so you may want to experiment with this setting to get it working just how you want it.

6. The **RSS settings** will consist of the following:

   ○ **Include RSS links**: This setting will show little RSS icons next to any pages that have RSS feeds. This is a great idea if you want people to be able to subscribe to your site's content.

   ○ **RSS feed depth**: This setting allows you to specify how many subcategories should display the RSS symbol. Dozens or hundreds of RSS symbols can get annoying so use your best judgment based on your site's content. Not sure? Just leave it on **all**.

7. Click on **Save configuration**.

8. Double check to make sure that your sitemap looks correct, by pointing your browser to `http://www.yourDrupalsite.com/sitemap`. Your sitemap should look similar to the following screenshot:

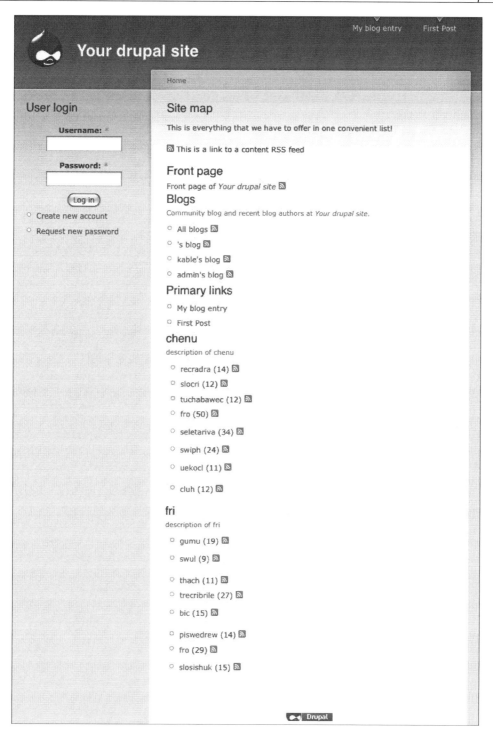

9. By default, your sitemap is only visible to the admin. You need to give permission to anonymous users to view the sitemap.

   ° Visit the following link, `http://www.yourDrupalsite.com/admin/user/permissions` or navigate to **Administer | User management | Permissions**.

   ° Next to **access site map**, check the box under **anonymous user** and **authenticated user**.

Permission	anonymous user	authenticated user
site_map module		
access site map	☑	☑

   ° Click on **Save permissions**.

Use the Devel module

I used the Devel module to generate some dummy data to see how the Site map module would look. Don't use Devel on a live site unless you really know what you're doing! However, when developing your site on a test server, the Devel module can be invaluable. Check it out: `http://drupal.org/project/devel`. Devel is maintained by the seemingly-ubiquitous Moshe Weitzman. He's a true Drupal Rockstar. Thanks, Moshe!

Summary

In this chapter, we discussed the origin of sitemaps and how they're used to make sure your entire site is crawled by the search engines. We also talked about how to make a user-friendly sitemap for your site visitors. In this chapter, we have covered the following topics:

- XML sitemaps
- URL-list sitemap
- Google News XML sitemaps
- Visitor-facing sitemaps

In the next chapter, it's time to get technical with your SEO. Get ready to face the robots!

6
robots.txt, .htaccess, and W3C Validation

Much of the SEO that we've accomplished so far is visible to your visitors (for example, titles, headings, body text, and even a sitemap or two). In this chapter, we're going to address some of the more technical aspects of on-page SEO. Over the last ten years, many elements have been added to the HTML specification. The search engines themselves have developed other elements to help you communicate better with them. Since our ultimate goal is to do well by the search engines and our visitors, it's time to embrace your inner geek and get technical with your SEO. Pocket protectors ready? Let's do this thing.

In this chapter, we're going to cover:

- The `robots.txt` files and common directives used in these files
- Problems with Drupal's standard `robots.txt` and how to fix them
- Adding the XML Sitemap to the `robots.txt`
- Understanding and editing the `.htaccess` file
- W3C Validation

Take care when upgrading your Drupal installation!

In this chapter, we discuss making edits to two different files that are considered **core** Drupal. Core means part of the base installation of Drupal and not in the /sites directory. While what you'll accomplish in this chapter is not considered **hacking core**, it does mean that when you upgrade your Drupal site (say from 6.14 to 6.15) you will need to preserve your robots.txt and .htaccess files so you don't overwrite them with the updated files. A bit complicated, yes, but it's well worth the effort the edits suggested here will bring to your SEO campaign.

Optimizing the robots.txt file

The robots.txt file is a file that sits at the root level of your web site and asks spiders and bots to behave themselves when they're on your site. You can take a look at it by pointing your browser to http://www.yourDrupalsite.com/robots. txt. Think of it like an electronic **No Trespassing** sign that can easily tell the search engines not to crawl a certain directory or page of your site. Using wildcards, you can even tell the engines not to crawl certain file types like .jpg or .pdf. This means none of your JPEG images or PDF files will show up in the search engines. (I'm not recommending that you do that...but you could.)

The robots.txt file is required by Google

On December 1, 2008, John Mueller, a Google analyst, said that if the Googlebot can't access the robots.txt file (say the server is unreachable or returns a 5xx error result code) then it won't crawl the web site at all. In other words, the robots.txt file must be there if you want the web site to be crawled and indexed by Google. Read his full comment at the following link: http://budURL.com/robotstxt.

Drupal 6 provides a standard robots.txt file that does an OK job. It looks like this:

```
# $Id: robots.txt,v 1.9.2.1 2008/12/10 20:12:19 goba Exp $
#
# robots.txt
#
# This file is to prevent the crawling and indexing of certain parts
# of your site by web crawlers and spiders run by sites like Yahoo!
# and Google. By telling these "robots" where not to go on your site,
# you save bandwidth and server resources.
#
# This file will be ignored unless it is at the root of your host:
# Used:    http://example.com/robots.txt
# Ignored: http://example.com/site/robots.txt
#
# For more information about the robots.txt standard, see:
# http://www.robotstxt.org/wc/robots.html
#
# For syntax checking, see:
# http://www.sxw.org.uk/computing/robots/check.html

User-agent: *
Crawl-delay: 10
# Directories
Disallow: /includes/
Disallow: /misc/
Disallow: /modules/
Disallow: /profiles/
Disallow: /scripts/
Disallow: /sites/
Disallow: /themes/
# Files
Disallow: /CHANGELOG.txt
Disallow: /cron.php
Disallow: /INSTALL.mysql.txt
Disallow: /INSTALL.pgsql.txt
Disallow: /install.php
Disallow: /INSTALL.txt
Disallow: /LICENSE.txt
Disallow: /MAINTAINERS.txt
Disallow: /update.php
Disallow: /UPGRADE.txt
Disallow: /xmlrpc.php
# Paths (clean URLs)
Disallow: /admin/
Disallow: /comment/reply/
Disallow: /contact/
Disallow: /logout/
Disallow: /node/add/
Disallow: /search/
Disallow: /user/register/
Disallow: /user/password/
Disallow: /user/login/
# Paths (no clean URLs)
Disallow: /?q=admin/
Disallow: /?q=comment/reply/
Disallow: /?q=contact/
Disallow: /?q=logout/
Disallow: /?q=node/add/
Disallow: /?q=search/
Disallow: /?q=user/password/
Disallow: /?q=user/register/
Disallow: /?q=user/login/
```

The Drupal 6 `robots.txt` file carries instructions for robots and spiders that may crawl your site.

robots.txt directives

Let's take a deeper look at each directive used in the Drupal `robots.txt` file. This is a bit tedious, but it's truly worth it to understand exactly what you're telling the search engines to do.

Robots.txt command	What it looks like	What it does
Comment	`#`	Hides text from the robot. This is a good way to put in notes or comments.
User Agent	`User-agent: *`	Tells which robot should read the following instructions. * means all robots.
Crawl Delay	`Crawl-delay: X`	The delay, in seconds, between page request from a bot. Replace X with a whole number between 1 and 20. Note that this directive is ignored by Google. You can adjust the crawl delay by using Google's Webmaster Tools.
Disallow	`Disallow: /path/` `Disallow: file.` `txt`	Says to the robots, 'Don't crawl this!'. In the case of paths, it won't crawl anything in that directory or below it.

Pattern matching

Google (but not all search engines) understands some wildcard characters. The following table explains the usage of a few wildcard characters:

To do this	Use this	Example
match a sequence of characters	`*`	`Disallow: /dev*/` will exclude any subdirectory that begins with the letters "dev".
block access to all URLs that include a X	`*`	`Disallow: /*?` (Preferred) is the same as `Disallow: /*?*` They both will disallow any path with a ? in it.
Specify a three letter extension at the end of any file	`*` and `$`	`Disallow: /*pdf$` will exclude any files that end with pdf across your entire site. However, it allows any file with pdf in the middle of the filename like `pdfdocslist.php`

To find out more, visit the following link:

```
http://www.google.com/support/webmasters/bin/
answer.py?hl=en&answer=40360#4
```

Editing your robots.txt file

Later in this chapter, you'll learn several changes that you'll need to make to your robots.txt file. Come back to this section to walk through the steps when you want to make each change.

1. Check to see if your robots.txt file is there and available to visiting search bots. Open your browser and visit the following link:
    http://www.yourDrupalsite.com/robots.txt

2. Using your FTP program or command line editor, navigate to the top level of your Drupal web site and locate the robots.txt file.

If , for some reason the robots.txt file is missing you can easily create one, using any plain text editor like Notepad or TextEdit. Avoid using a word processor, though, as they add additional content which will make the file unreadable to the search engines.

3. Make a backup of the file.

4. Open the robots.txt file for editing. If necessary, download the file and open it in a local text editor tool.

5. Most directives in the robots.txt file are based on the line User-agent:. If you are going to give different instructions to different engines, be sure to place them above the User-agent: *, as some search engines will only read the directives for * if you place their specific instructions following that section.

6. Add the lines you want. Later in this chapter, you'll learn several changes which will help you with your SEO.

7. Save your robots.txt file, uploading it if necessary, replacing the existing file (you backed it up, didn't you?).

8. Point your browser to http://www.yourDrupalsite.com/robots.txt and double-check that your changes are in effect. You may need to do a refresh on your browser to see the changes.

Problems with the default Drupal robots.txt file

There are several problems with the default Drupal robots.txt file. If you use Google Webmaster Tool's robots.txt testing utility (detailed instructions on this utility later in this chapter) to test each line of the file, you'll find that a lot of paths which look like they're being blocked will actually be crawled. The reason is that Drupal does not require the trailing slash (/) after the path to show you the content. Because of the way robots.txt files are parsed, **Googlebot** will avoid the page with the slash but crawl the page without the slash.

 Google what? Googlebot! Google and other search engines use server systems (sometimes called spiders, crawlers, or robots) to go around the Internet and find each web site. We sometimes refer to Google's system as the Googlebot to distinguish it from other search engine robots. While Google doesn't report this number anymore, it is estimated that the Googlebot crawls 10 billion web sites each week! That is a fast little robot.

For example, /admin/ is listed as disallowed. As you would expect, the testing utility shows that http://www.yourDrupalsite.com/admin/ is disallowed. But, put in http://www.yourDrupalsite.com/admin (without the trailing slash) and you'll see that it is allowed. Disaster! Fortunately, this is relatively easy to fix.

Fixing the Drupal robots.txt file

Carry out the following steps in order to fix the Drupal robots.txt file:

1. Make a backup of the robots.txt file.

2. Open the robots.txt file for editing. If necessary, download the file and open it in a local text editor.

3. Find the Paths (clean URLs) section and the Paths (no clean URLs) section. Note that both sections appear whether you've turned on clean URLs or not. Drupal covers you either way. They look like this:

```
# Paths (clean URLs)
Disallow: /admin/
Disallow: /comment/reply/
Disallow: /contact/
Disallow: /logout/
Disallow: /node/add/
Disallow: /search/
Disallow: /user/register/
```

```
Disallow: /user/password/
Disallow: /user/login/
# Paths (no clean URLs)
Disallow: /?q=admin/
Disallow: /?q=comment/reply/
Disallow: /?q=contact/
Disallow: /?q=logout/
Disallow: /?q=node/add/
Disallow: /?q=search/
Disallow: /?q=user/password/
Disallow: /?q=user/register/
Disallow: /?q=user/login/
```

4. Duplicate the two sections (simply copy and paste them) so that you have four sections — two of the `# Paths (clean URLs)` sections and two of `# Paths (no clean URLs)` sections.

5. Add `'fixed!'` to the comment of the new sections so that you can tell them apart.

6. Delete the trailing / after each `Disallow` line in the `fixed!` sections. You should end up with four sections that look like this:

```
# Paths (clean URLs)
Disallow: /admin/
Disallow: /comment/reply/
Disallow: /contact/
Disallow: /logout/
Disallow: /node/add/
Disallow: /search/
Disallow: /user/register/
Disallow: /user/password/
Disallow: /user/login/
# Paths (no clean URLs)
Disallow: /?q=admin/
Disallow: /?q=comment/reply/
Disallow: /?q=contact/
Disallow: /?q=logout/
Disallow: /?q=node/add/
Disallow: /?q=search/
Disallow: /?q=user/password/
Disallow: /?q=user/register/
```

```
Disallow: /?q=user/login/
# Paths (clean URLs) - fixed!
Disallow: /admin
Disallow: /comment/reply
Disallow: /contact
Disallow: /logout
Disallow: /node/add
Disallow: /search
Disallow: /user/register
Disallow: /user/password
Disallow: /user/login
# Paths (no clean URLs) - fixed!
Disallow: /?q=admin
Disallow: /?q=comment/reply
Disallow: /?q=contact
Disallow: /?q=logout
Disallow: /?q=node/add
Disallow: /?q=search
Disallow: /?q=user/password
Disallow: /?q=user/register
Disallow: /?q=user/login
```

7. Save your `robots.txt file`, uploading it if necessary, replacing the existing file (you backed it up, didn't you?).

8. Go to `http://www.yourDrupalsite.com/robots.txt` and double-check that your changes are in effect. You may need to do a refresh on your browser to see the changes.

Now your `robots.txt` file is working as you would expect it to.

Additional changes to the robots.txt file

Using directives and pattern matching commands, the `robots.txt` file can exclude entire sections of the site from the crawlers like the admin pages, certain individual files like `cron.php`, and some directories like `/scripts` and `/modules`.

In many cases, though, you should tweak your `robots.txt` file for optimal SEO results. Here are several changes you can make to the file to meet your needs in certain situations:

- You are developing a new site and you don't want it to show up in any search engine until you're ready to launch it. Add `Disallow: *` just after the `User-agent:`

- Say you're running a very slow server and you don't want the crawlers to slow your site down for other users. Adjust the `Crawl-delay` by changing it from 10 to 20.

- If you're on a super-fast server (and you should be, right?) you can tell the bots to bring it on! Change the `Crawl-delay` to 5 or even 1 second. Monitor your server closely for a few days to make sure it can handle the extra load.

- Say you're running a site which allows people to upload their own images but you don't necessarily want those images to show up in Google. Add these lines at the bottom of your `robots.txt` file:

```
User-agent: Googlebot-Image
Disallow: /*.jpg$
Disallow: /*.gif$
Disallow: /*.png$
```

  If all of the files were in the `/files/users/images/` directory, you could do this:

```
User-agent: Googlebot-Image
Disallow: /files/users/images/
```

- Say you noticed in your server logs that there was a bad robot out there that was scraping all your content. You can try to prevent this by adding this to the bottom of your `robots.txt` file:

```
User-agent: Bad-Robot
Disallow: *
```

Bad robots, renegade spiders, killer crawlers—it sounds like the plot of a 1950s sci-fi but they're real and they can hurt your site. Mostly, they just pull server resources and bandwidth away from your server. However, they could be doing other things like stealing your content or even spamming your users. The `robots.txt` file is your way of saying, 'No, robot! That's a bad robot! No scraps for you!'. It may help but you may need to get serious and have your server administrator deny service to the bots based on identifying string or IP address. Just be careful not to block all of the bots as your site will stop showing up in Google.

- If you have installed the XML Sitemap module, then you've got a great tool that you should send out to all of the search engines. However, it's tedious to go to each engine's site and upload your URL. Instead, you can add a couple of simple lines to the `robots.txt` file. For more information, see the section called Adding your XML Sitemap to the robots.txt file, later in this chapter.

> **robots.txt is a request, not a command**
>
> Do not expect that just because you put it in the `robots.txt` file that it will be strictly obeyed. Rogue spiders and bots often ignore your requests. This is highly unlikely from the major search engines, but it can, and does, happen. With this in mind, if you really want to obscure sensitive documents from the rest of the world, put it behind a password-protected section of your site.

Adding your XML Sitemap to the robots.txt file

Another way that that the `robots.txt` file helps you search engine optimize your Drupal site is by allowing you to specify where your sitemaps are located. While you probably want to submit your sitemap directly to Google, Yahoo!, and MSN, it's a good idea to put a reference to it in the `robots.txt` file for all of those other search engines. You can do this by carrying out the following steps:

1. Open the `robots.txt` file for editing.

2. The sitemap directive is independent of the `User-agent` line, so it doesn't matter where you place it in your `robots.txt` file.

   ○ To keep things neat, add this line first:
   ```
   # Sitemaps
   ```

   ○ Add these lines for your XML sitemap:
   ```
   Sitemap: http://www.yourDrupalsite.com/sitemap.xml
   Sitemap: http://www.yourDrupalsite.com/
   ?q=sitemap.xml
   ```

   ○ If you're using the URL list sitemap instead, add these lines:
   ```
   Sitemap: http://www.yourDrupalsite.com/urllist.txt
   Sitemap: http://www.yourDrupalsite.com/?q=urllist.
   txt
   ```

3. Your finished `robots.txt` file should look similar to the following screenshot:

```
# http://www.sxw.org.uk/computing/robots/check.html

# Sitemaps
Sitemap: http://www.yourdrupalsite.com/sitemap.xml
Sitemap: http://www.yourdrupalsite.com/?q=sitemap.xml

User-agent: *
Crawl-delay: 10
# Directories
```

4. Save your `robots.txt` file, uploading it if necessary, replacing the existing file (you backed it up, didn't you?).

5. Go to `http://www.yourDrupalsite.com/robots.txt` and double-check that your changes are in effect. You may need to perform a refresh on your browser to see the changes.

 If you have an XML sitemap, use it. If not, use the URL list sitemap. However, do not add both, an XML sitemap and a URL list sitemap, to the `robots.txt` file. It could confuse the search engines; possibly even causing duplicate content on your site. Also, do not add your visitor-facing sitemap to your `robots.txt` file.

Using Google's Webmaster Tools to evaluate your robots.txt file

Warning! The `robots.txt` file is easy to mess up! It's not written for humans so it's easy for site owners and webmasters to misunderstand exactly how to use it. Take care not to break your SEO campaign simply because a poorly written `robots.txt` file is excluding your site from Google. Fortunately, Google's Webmaster Tools provides a helpful utility that shows you exactly which pages are being excluded and included by your `robots.txt` file. Carry out the following steps to evaluate your `robots.txt` file using Google's Webmaster Tools:

1. Go to `http://www.google.com/webmasters/`, log in, and click on your site.

2. Click on the **Tools** menu item and you'll see a screen similar to the following screenshot:

3. Click on **Analyze robots.txt**. You'll see some interesting statistics about your `robots.txt` file that looks similar to the following screenshot:

You'll see the following options on the next page:

- ○ **URL**: The location of your file
- ○ **Last downloaded**: The last snapshot that Google took of your robots.txt file. They tend to grab the latest file once per day.
- ○ **Status**: Anything other than 200 (Success) means that there's a problem with your robots.txt file.
- ○ **Parsing results**: Indicates any lines or rules that are ignored by Google. As you can see in this example, Google is ignoring the crawl-delay.

4. Further down the page, you'll see the text of the `robot.txt` file that Google last downloaded from your site. If you've tweaked it more recently than the last download, you can copy and paste your changes into the box provided so that you can test your changes. This is for testing purposes only. Any changes you make will not be saved.

5. The next box, labeled Test URLs against this `robots.txt` file, is a list of URLs from your web site. By making changes to the `robots.txt` box and adding URLs, you can see how different rules will affect the way Google sees your site.

6. Further down, **Choose User-agents** allows you to specify which Googlebot you want to evaluate. Google has several they use, like Googlebot-Mobile and Googlebot-Image.

Let's try an example. We're going to tell Googlebot-Image to leave our site alone! As you can see below, I added these lines to the `robots.txt` text box:

```
User-agent: Googlebot-Image
Disallow: /*.jpg$
Disallow: /*.gif$
Disallow: /*.png$
```

I also added the site logo file into the **Test URLs** box:

```
http://www.yourDrupalsite.com/themes/garland/logo.png
```

I chose Googlebot-Image as the Googlebot and here's what it looks like:

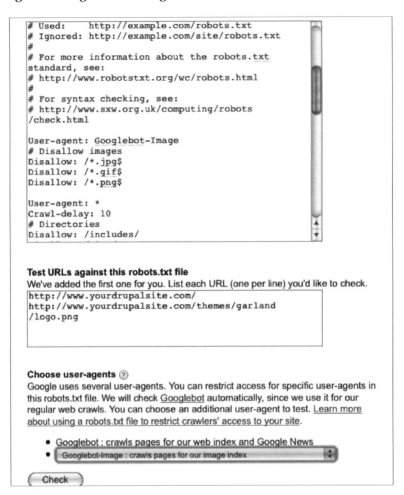

When I click on **Check**, here's what I see:

URL results		
URL	Googlebot	Googlebot-Image
http://www.yourdrupalsite.com/	Allowed	Allowed
http://www.yourdrupalsite.com/themes/garland/logo.png	Blocked by line 35: Disallow: /themes/	Blocked by line 24: Disallow: /*.png$

Parsing results	
Value	Result
Line 27 : Crawl-delay: 10	Rule ignored by Googlebot

Success! Both Googlebot and Googlebot-Image were blocked by our `robots.txt` file.

> For more information about the `robots.txt` specification,
> please visit these sites:
>
> `http://www.robotstxt.org/`
>
> `http://www.google.com/support/webmasters/bin/`
> `answer.py?answer=40360&hl=en`
>
> `http://tips.webdesign10.com/robots-txt-and-drupal`

Feel free to try different things on your own. You can't hurt your site here. If you like what you've done, be sure to copy and paste the changes into the `robots.txt` file on the root level of your Drupal site.

Mastering the .htaccess file

There is a server configuration file at the root level of your Drupal 6 site called the `.htaccess` file. This file is a list of instructions to your web server software, usually Apache. These instructions are very helpful for cleaning up some redirects and otherwise making your site function a bit better for the search engines. In Chapter 1, *The Tools You'll Need*, we told Google Webmaster Tools that we wanted our site to show up in Google with or without the **www** in the URL. The `.htaccess` file allows you to do the same thing directly on your web site. Why are both necessary? In Google's tool, you're only telling Google how you want them to display your URLs; you're not actually changing the URLs on your web site. With the `.htaccess` file, you're actually affecting how the files are served. This will change how your site is displayed in all search engines.

> **Hey, why can't I can't see the .htaccess file?**
>
> In Unix/Linux Operating Systems, any file that begins with a period (.) is considered an invisible file. This means the `.htaccess` file wouldn't normally show up when you're viewing files on your server. Many FTP programs respect this standard and by default won't show you the files. If you want to see them, look in your FTP program's settings or preferences for **Show hidden files**, and make sure that it's set to show you those files. You may need to restart your FTP program and refresh the file list before you will see the `.htaccess` file.

Carry out the following steps to master the .htaccess file:

1. Back up your .htaccess file. (It's really easy to mess it up.) Duplicate it and rename the new file to htaccess.txt or something similar.

2. Open your .htaccess file for editing. You'll be able to see a screen similar to the following screenshot:

```
#
# Apache/PHP/Drupal settings:
#

# Protect files and directories from prying eyes.
<FilesMatch "\.(engine|inc|info|install|module|profile|test|po|sh|.*sql|theme|
tpl(\.php)?|xtmpl|svn-base)$|^(code-style\.pl|Entries.*|Repository|Root|Tag|
Template|all-wcprops|entries|format)$">
  Order allow,deny
</FilesMatch>

# Don't show directory listings for URLs which map to a directory.
Options -Indexes

# Follow symbolic links in this directory.
Options +FollowSymLinks

# Make Drupal handle any 404 errors.
ErrorDocument 404 /index.php

# Force simple error message for requests for non-existent favicon.ico.
<Files favicon.ico>
  # There is no end quote below, for compatibility with Apache 1.3.
  ErrorDocument 404 "The requested file favicon.ico was not found.
</Files>

# Set the default handler.
DirectoryIndex index.php

# Override PHP settings. More in sites/default/settings.php
# but the following cannot be changed at runtime.

# PHP 4, Apache 1.
<IfModule mod_php4.c>
```

3. Scroll to the bottom of the file and you should see a block of text that looks like this. I've highlighted the 4 lines you should be concerned with:

```
# If your site can be accessed both with and without the
  'www.' prefix, you
# can use one of the following settings to redirect users to
  your preferred
# URL, either WITH or WITHOUT the 'www.' prefix. Choose ONLY one
  option:
#
# To redirect all users to access the site WITH the 'www.'
prefix,
```

```
# (http://example.com/... will be redirected to
  http://www.example.com/...)
# adapt and uncomment the following:
# RewriteCond %{HTTP_HOST} ^example\.com$ [NC]
# RewriteRule ^(.*)$ http://www.example.com/$1 [L,R=301]
#
# To redirect all users to access the site WITHOUT the 'www.'
  prefix,
# (http://www.example.com/... will be redirected to
  http://example.com/...)
# uncomment and adapt the following:
# RewriteCond %{HTTP_HOST} ^www\.example\.com$ [NC]
# RewriteRule ^(.*)$ http://example.com/$1 [L,R=301]
```

4. The following table will help you deal with the redirection of the URLs:

To do this	Make this change	Example
Redirect non-www URLs to www	Remove the # from the first two highlighted lines	`http://example.com` will redirect to `http://www.example.com`
Redirect www URLs to non-www	Remove the # from the last two highlighted lines	`http://www.example.com` will redirect to `http://example.com`

5. Save the `.htaccess` file and, if necessary, upload it to the server.

6. Test your site! If there is a problem, restore from your backup `.htaccess` file.

7. Don't forget to tell Google which you prefer using Google Webmaster Tools. See the Google Webmaster Tools section in Chapter 1, *The Tools You'll Need*, for more infomation on how to do this.

W3C markup validation

Drupal is a well-written piece of software that produces well-formed web sites. However, don't assume that it will still be that way when you're done with it. Not all of the modules, themes, or content on your site will pass muster. This is especially true if your site is open to users to create their own content.

You should run a comprehensive scan of the site to check for improperly formed code, broken links, and other oversights that could hinder your search engine positioning. Obviously, Google can't reject sites just because they have bad markup (most of the sites out there have at least one thing wrong with them). However, bad HTML can confuse the search engine spiders. They're not as forgiving as a modern browser is to technical issues. By eliminating any problem markup, you can remove this concern from your site.

There is a great, and free, tool that you can use to scan your site. It's called the **W3C HTML Validator**.

Scanning your site with the W3C HTML Validator

Carry out the following steps to scan your site with the W3C HTML Validator:

1. Go to `http://validator.w3.org/`. You will see a screen similar to the following screenshot:

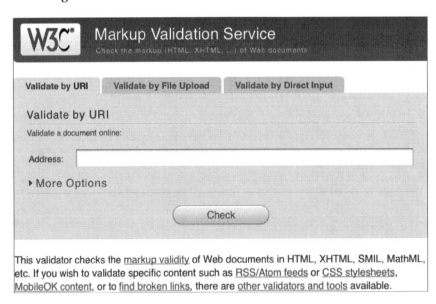

2. Paste your URL in the **Address** box and click on the **Check** button.

3. If your site passes validation, you should see a success message, as shown in the following screenshot:

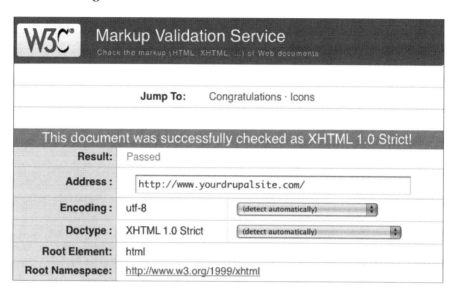

4. If your site does not validate, you'll see a message and a list of suggested fixes, as shown in the following screenshot:

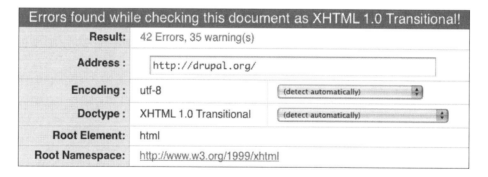

5. Fortunately, W3C outputs a comprehensive list of the problems, and even suggests how to fix them, as shown in the following screenshot:

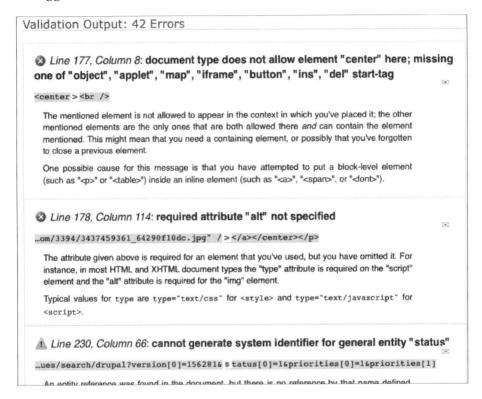

6. Fix the problems and resubmit.

Now that you have your site 100% compliant, you can be rest assured that the search engine bots will not be confused by bad markup the next time they come crawling.

Summary

In this chapter, we covered some of the most technical aspects of a good SEO. We discussed:

- The robots.txt file
- The .htaccess files
- W3C Validation

We've got one more chapter of technical, on-page optimization, and then you'll be ready to start populating your site with content.

7

RSS Feeds, Site Speed, and SEO Testing

If you've followed along chapter by chapter through this book, then you have a very well optimized Drupal web site at this point. There are only a couple of things left to do and you'll be finished with the on-page optimization. You've come this far, so let's finish it strong. We're going to talk about RSS feeds, optimizing your site's PageRank, tweaking your site speed, and testing your site's quality and optimization score with some third party services. While it could be said that these things are optional, I've found that the difference between the top 10 and number 1 in Google is how well you take care of all of the little details. It merits saying again, the great thing about Drupal is that you set these things up one time and they're (almost) done forever.

In this chapter, we're going to cover:

- RSS feeds
- The Syndication module
- Speeding up your site
- The SEOmoz's free Page Grading Service

Setting up RSS feeds

Ever seen an icon, similar to the following screenshot, on the web, before?

These icons are indicators that the site's owner wants to share his content with you. If you ever subscribe to a podcast, or read a blog in a newsreader, then you've used an **RSS feed**. RSS is a standard way of sharing your Drupal web site without visitors needing to come back to your site each day (or hour, or minute) to check if you have new content.

 RSS stands for **Really Simple Syndication** or **Rich Site Summary**, depending on who you ask. It was created by Ramanathan V. Guha, Dan Libby, and Dave Winer in the late 1990s, and has become a standard for sites that have frequently updated content.

Users subscribe to your RSS feed in their own newsreader. Periodically, the newsreader automatically checks the RSS feed to see if there is any new content there. If there is new content, the newsreader downloads a summary of the article and alerts the user that there is new content. If that person is interested in reading the entire article, then they click on the summary which launches their browser and displays your web site. The magic of RSS has brought a visitor back to your site.

Technically, an RSS feed is a standardized way of communicating content using XML. It looks as follows (from `http://drupal.org/node/feed`):

```
<?xml version="1.0" encoding="utf-8"?>
<rss version="2.0" xml:base="http://drupal.org"  xmlns:dc="http://
purl.org/dc/elements/1.1/">
<channel>
 <title>drupal.org</title>
 <link>http://drupal.org</link>
 <description>Drupal.org is the official web site of Drupal, an open
source content management platform.  Equipped with a powerful blend of
features, Drupal supports a variety of web sites ranging from personal
weblogs to large community-driven web sites.</description>
 <language>en</language>
<item>
 <title>Drupal 6.11 and 5.17 released</title>
 <link>http://drupal.org/drupal-6.11</link>
 <description>&lt;div style=&quot;float: right; padding: 0.8em;
background-color: #0174BB; font-size: 1.2em; margin: 0 0 0.3em 0.3em;
text-align: center;&quot;&gt;&lt;a
 </description>
```

And so on.

Lucky for us, one of the coolest things about RSS in Drupal is that we never need to worry about creating these feeds ourselves. Almost any list of nodes in Drupal has an RSS feed associated with it. Your main page has an RSS feed that has every node published in it. If you created category pages, then there are RSS feeds automatically created for those pages. Even pages created with the Views module have RSS feeds associated with them. However, all of these RSS feeds are hidden from view. If you know they're there, then you can make use of them. However, if your visitors can't see them, then they can't subscribe to your site's content.

Fortunately, there's a great module that will help you show your RSS feeds to your users. This lets them take advantage of all your site has to offer. It's called **Syndication**, and it's another fine module from Moshe Weitzman. Thanks again, Moshe!

Setting up the Syndication module

Carry out the following steps to set up the Syndication module:

1. Download the Syndication module from the following link,
    `http://drupal.org/project/syndication` and install it just like a normal
    Drupal module. Refer to Chapter 1, *The Tools You'll Need*, for step-by-step
    module installation instructions.

2. Go to `http://www.yourDrupalsite.com/admin/content/syndication`, or go to your admin screen and click on the **Administer | Content Management | RSS feed syndication** link. You'll see the **RSS feed syndication** screen, as shown in the following screenshot:

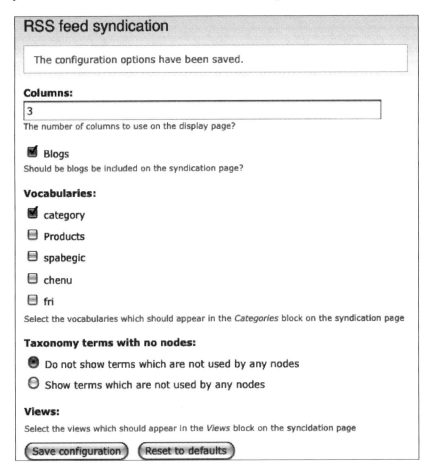

3. Enter the number of columns you would like to have displayed on the syndication page.

4. Select **Blogs** if you would like each user's blog RSS feed to show up on the syndication page.

5. Under **Vocabularies**, select the category that you would like to show up on the syndication page.

6. You probably should leave the **Taxonomy terms with no nodes** option, set at the default of **Do not show terms which are not used by any nodes**.

7. Click on **Save configuration**.

8. Visit the following link: `http://www.yourDrupalsite.com/syndication`. You should see a screen similar to the following screenshot:

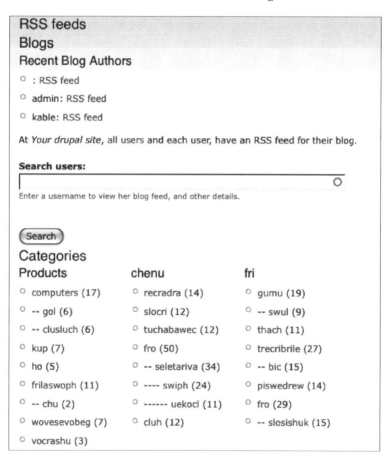

What about pages that aren't listed here?

Add /feed to any Drupal page to find out if there is a feed for that page. For example, if the URL of a page on your Drupal site is:

`http://www.yourDrupalsite.com/blog`

change it to:

`http://www.yourDrupalsite.com/blog/feed`

and you'll see the RSS feed for that page.

Adding RSS links to your blog

Both the Site map and the Syndication modules add blocks which display your RSS feeds. It's a good idea to add this block to your blog pages. You can add them to all of the pages if you feel that would be helpful to your visitors. Carry out the following steps to add RSS links to your blog:

1. If you don't have the Site map or Syndication modules installed, install one of them now.

2. Go to `http://www.yourDrupalsite.com/admin/build/block`, or navigate to **Administer | Site Building | Blocks**. You'll see a screen similar to the following screenshot:

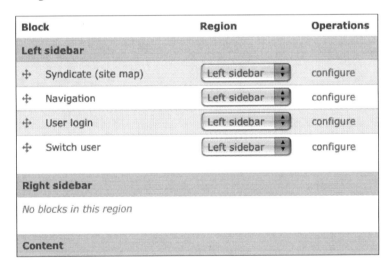

3. In the disabled block list, you'll see three different Syndication blocks.

4. Pick the one that says **Syndicate (site map)** and put it into one of the active regions on your site.

5. Click on **Save blocks**.

6. Now, click on the **configure** link, located next to the newly active **Syndicate (site map)** block. You should see a screen similar to the following screenshot:

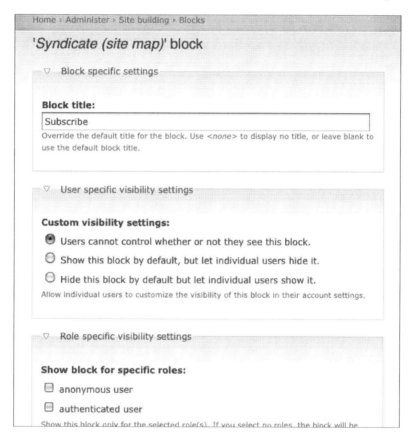

The preceding screenshot is the upper half of the Syndicate configure screen. The bottom half of the Syndicate configure screen is shown in the following screenshot:

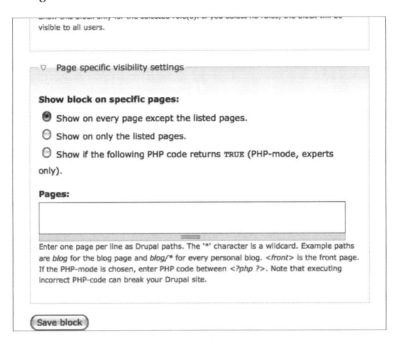

7. Change the **Block title** to **Subscribe, RSS,** or something more meaningful than **Syndicate**.

8. Under the **Show block on specific pages** option, change the selection to **Show on only the listed pages** and enter the following text: ***blog* The asterisk acts as a wildcard and will cause the block to show on any page that has the word blog in the path.**

9. Click on the **Save block** option. Your page will look similar to the following screenshot:

Feel the need—the need for speed

Waiting around for a web site to load is like watching paint dry. It's boring and it makes me nauseous. I can only put up with it if I really, really want the information the site has to offer. Everyone who visits your web site feels the same way. Give them what they're looking for quickly and you stand a better chance of meeting their needs and closing the deal. Like slow service in a restaurant, people may stick around, but they're probably not going to be back anytime soon.

Google likes fast web sites, too. Think about it from their perspective: all things being equal, a quick and peppy web site will make a user happier than a slow web site. There are other considerations for Google as well. For example, when they send around their spider, how quickly can your server give over the data they're looking for?

Fortunately, Drupal has some cool, built-in ways to speed up your site without having to invest in expensive server hardware and hosting.

Turning on Drupal's built-in caching

Thanks to browsers, most people know what caching is. If you go to a web site once, Firefox and other modern browsers will keep a snapshot of that page for a while so that if you hit the **Back** button, it instantly loads the page. Servers can do that as well. When someone visits a page, the server will cache and compress it. When a second person visits the same page, the server can send the cached page instead of going back to the database. It's much faster and saves bandwidth.

Drupal has its own caching mechanism built right in. If enabled, it will take a snapshot of the static parts of your Drupal web site (like the blocks, header, and CSS files), compress them, and serve them whenever someone asks for those things. This is much faster because your Drupal site would normally need to perform a lot of PHP and database calculations to construct each page for each person. Now, it can just serve the cached file to everyone and avoid the extra work each time.

 Wait until your site is done with development before you turn caching on, though, because it will delay many changes to the site files. For example, edits to the theme CSS files may not show up immediately.

Carry out the following steps in order to turn on Drupal's built-in caching:

1. Go to `http://www.yourDrupalsite.com/admin/settings/performance`, or navigate to **Administer | Site Configuration | Performance**. You'll see a screen similar to the following screenshot:

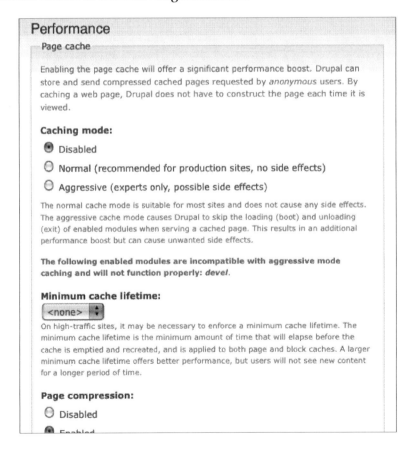

2. There are three sections here, each one speeds up your site in some way:

Page cache

○ Under **Caching Mode**, select **Normal**. This will dramatically speed up your site for anonymous visitors but Drupal will continue to show the freshest content to logged-in visitors. This works very well for sites that have a lot of visitors from the search engines or other sources.

○ **Minimum cache lifetime** is probably left alone for most sites. However, if you have a high-traffic site and are still encountering performance issues, try increasing this setting. Just remember that if you have this turned on, that is the minimum amount of time before new content will show up.

○ **Page compression:** This will compress the cached pages so that they download faster to each user. It's best turned on unless you know that your web server already performs this function. Most hosting companies do not.

Block cache: It does just what it sounds like. It caches the contents of all of the blocks on your Drupal site. This helps all users, not just anonymous ones, so this is a great option if you have a social networking or forum web site. Select the **Enabled** option.

○ **Bandwidth optimizations**: You may need to visit the link, `http://www.yourDrupalsite.com/admin/settings/file-system` and turn on the **Public** download method for these two site optimizations to work.

○ **Optimize CSS files**: It aggregates and compresses your CSS files into one. Depending on which theme and modules you have installed, this could pull in 10 to 15 different CSS files, saving the server a lot of file system calls each time a page loads. Set to **Enabled** when you're finished with site development.

○ **Optimize Javascript files** aggregates (but does not compress) all of the Javascript files on your site. This also helps to keep the server efficient by saving multiple calls to the file system. Set to **Enabled** when you're finished with site development.

Clear cached data: Use this option when you've made changes to your site and you want to clear out the cached files. This helps when troubleshooting site development, themes, and modules. Just remember that your site will slow down for several minutes while the cached files are rebuilt. If your site is functioning normally, it is not necessary to use **Clear cached data**.

3. Click on **Save configuration**.

You can see parts of the caching in action by viewing the page source before and after you turn caching on. Before, the JavaScript and CSS source of your home page looked similar to the following screenshot:

```
Source of: http://www.yourdrupalsite.com/
<title>Your drupal site | </title>
<link type="text/css" rel="stylesheet" media="all"
href="/sites/all/modules/admin_menu/admin_menu.css?P" />
<link type="text/css" rel="stylesheet" media="all"
href="/modules/node/node.css?P" />
<link type="text/css" rel="stylesheet" media="all"
href="/modules/system/defaults.css?P" />
<link type="text/css" rel="stylesheet" media="all"
href="/modules/system/system.css?P" />
<link type="text/css" rel="stylesheet" media="all"
href="/modules/system/system-menus.css?P" />
<link type="text/css" rel="stylesheet" media="all"
href="/modules/user/user.css?P" />
<link type="text/css" rel="stylesheet" media="all" href="/sites
/all/modules/elf/elf.css?P" />
<link type="text/css" rel="stylesheet" media="all" href="/themes
/garland/style.css?P" />
<link type="text/css" rel="stylesheet" media="print"
href="/themes/garland/print.css?P" />
    <script type="text/javascript" src="/misc/jquery.js?P">
</script>
<script type="text/javascript" src="/misc/drupal.js?P"></script>
<script type="text/javascript" defer="defer" src="/sites
/all/modules/admin_menu/admin_menu.js?P"></script>
<script type="text/javascript" src="/misc/autocomplete.js?P">
</script>
<script type="text/javascript" src="/misc/tableheader.js?P">
</script>
<script type="text/javascript">
<!--//--><![CDATA[//><!--
jQuery.extend(Drupal.settings, { "basePath": "/", "admin_menu":
{ "destination": "destination=node%2F1", "hash":
"a5df3eebfe98b0bfede7f4d43e1f97cb", "basePath": "/",
"replacements": { ".admin-menu-users a": "0 / 0" },
"margin_top": 1 } });
//--><!]]>
</script>
```

Do you see all of those calls to CSS and JavaScript files? Every time someone views your site in a browser, it's pulling in all of those files. After you turn on CSS and JavaScript optimization, your source will look more like this:

```
⬤⬤⬤                Source of: http://www.yourdrupalsite.com/        ⬯
    <title>Your drupal site | </title>
    <link type="text/css" rel="stylesheet" media="all"
href="/sites/all/modules/admin_menu/admin_menu.css?P" />
<link type="text/css" rel="stylesheet" media="all" href="/sites
/default/files/css/bcbd1c18543735141ea936d74578813c.css" />
<link type="text/css" rel="stylesheet" media="print"
href="/sites/default/files
/css/34e765e72d4819f40715b37a75e2d9a3.css" />
    <script type="text/javascript" src="/sites/default/files
/js/905f45b5bae30a8a358ed9ddce79553b.js"></script>
<script type="text/javascript">
<!--//--><![CDATA[//><!--
jQuery.extend(Drupal.settings, { "basePath": "/", "admin_menu":
{ "destination": "destination=node%2F1", "hash":
"a5df3eebfe98b0bfede7f4d43e1f97cb", "basePath": "/",
"replacements": { ".admin-menu-users a": "0 / 1" },
"margin_top": 1 } });
//--><![]]>
</script>
```

The fewer the number of files, the faster will be the server.

> **Content Refresh Module**
>
> If you allow anonymous users to post comments to your Drupal site,
> and you have caching turned on, then comments posted may not
> immediately show up because a cached version of the page is showing.
> Consider using the Content Refresh module (`http://drupal.org/
> project/content_refresh`). This module, created by Ramiro Gómez,
> automatically refreshes the page cache for that page when a user posts a
> comment. Sweet!

Now, your site should be noticeably quicker. However, if it's still not fast enough,
there are more things you can try.

More speed options

Let's face it. If you've done everything you can to speed up Drupal using its built-
in options, and it's still not performing, then you've got a good problem! But, it's a
problem that needs to be solved. Here are several additional things you can do:

- Look into modules that offer additional options for caching like Advanced
  cache, ApacheBench, Authenticated User Page Caching (Authcache), Block
  Cache Alter, Boost, Cache browser, Cache Router, JavaScript Aggregator,
  Memcache (Memcache is a popular choice if your host supports it or you're
  running your own server)
- If you're using a hosting company, ask to move to a faster server or
  switch companies

- Upgrade your server
- Upgrade your bandwidth
- Deploy Drupal to multiple servers
- Use PHP-level caching systems like Zend Platform

More speed help

There are dozens of pages on www.Drupal.org and other sites, dealing with all kinds of performance enhancements with Drupal. Visit the following link for more information: http://drupal.org/ node/326504. (Some of the performance ideas in this book came from that page.)

Bringing it all together with a free page grading service from SEOmoz

There are some free online tools that will help you evaluate how well you've built your site. The best one I've found, so far, is the SEOmoz Term Target. Carry out the following steps to use the free page grading service from SEOmoz:

1. Go to http://www.seomoz.org/tools (you may need to register for a free account first). Click on the **Term Target** link. You should see something like this:

2. Put in your page's URL and a keyword (one keyword) and click on **Grade My Term Targeting**. You will need to wait for about 30 seconds and then see your grade, (as seen in the following sample) screenshot:

Term Target Report

This report displays the result of your Term Targeting test. The purpose of this report is to give you an idea of how well your page is targeting a specific keyword and whether you can improve your targeting by incorporating the keyword in more strategic locations throughout the page. The report is broken down into a summary of term target factors and an extended analysis of term target elements and your keyword's prominence within those sections.

Your URL Grade

After analyzing your page for the supplied keyword's prominence, the Term Targeting tool will issue your page a letter grade (e.g. an A+ would mean that your keyword appears in 90-100% of our tool's parameters, while a C- signifies that your keyword appears in 50-54% of the tested elements). The higher the percentage, the better targeted your page is for the keyword you specified.

3. Anything less than an **A** needs more attention. Go through each of the recommendations listed and fix any issues with your site.

Summary

So, you've finally got all that pesky on-page optimization finished. Great job! You're done working on your site, right? Well, maintaining your on-page SEO is an ongoing task that is never quite done. Every new piece of content—be it a node, user, or comment—needs your attention. After you've worked through the recommendations so far in this book, your site will do a lot of the work for you, saving you a lot of time.

In this chapter, we have covered:

- RSS Feeds
- PageRank
- Drupal's built-in caching
- Checking your site with SEOmoz

Now that your site is search engine optimized, it's time to populate it with some great content.

8
Content is King

Search engines love content. They make their money by taking good content and serving it up to the masses. Think about it from Google's perspective. The better the content on your site, the happier the search engine user is going to be when they get there. Happy visitors will use Google again and again. The purpose of this chapter is to talk about ways that you can create fantastic content that the search engines will crawl, index, and then put in their search results. The more excellent the content on your site, the more visitors will find you. In this chapter, we're going to cover:

- What is good content
- How to write good content
- Search Engine Optimizing your content
- What to write about
- How to stay inspired
- Using Drupal to organize your content
- The right way to remove content from your site

What good content is

Good content is relevant, timely, interesting, and worth sharing with others. Content comes in many forms. It can be in the form of:

- Articles
- Videos
- Images
- Flash movies
- Comments
- Forum posts and much more

It's also the headlines, title, subtitles, and other helper text surrounding it.

At this point in the world of search engines, content is textual. Even if you create videos or images that are high quality, the search engines use the words—the text—around those media to decide what they are and how to categorize them. This means that the written word is far more important to search engines than any other kind of media.

We'll cover video and images a bit later. For now, let's talk about writing.

Write right

The first thing to remember about writing is that you need to write well; that is, use good grammar. Write in short, catchy ideas that get people interested in what you have to say. Write content that you yourself would love to read. This helps hold your audience's interest and gets them talking about, and linking to, your content. These are all things that will help you in the search engines.

Short, catchy headlines

Start your content with a short, catchy headline. The headline is the most obvious part of any piece of content that you create. It's what reaches out and grabs the reader and keeps them interested long enough to read the first couple of sentences. Remember, most Internet readers don't read, they skim. Therefore, it's important that your headline grabs the eye and the imagination.

If your headlines are weak, and your content can't carry the team, you have a major problem. Great headlines will not only increase traffic to your web site, but they will keep visitors coming back for more.

Grab their attention

You must make a promise with your headline, something that is relevant to your target audience. Speak to them directly. This seems obvious, but people still miss the mark. The best headlines are the ones that capture an entire idea in a few words. Think magazine covers or movie titles. Remember, your goal is to grab the attention. Here are some examples from the checkout at my local grocery store:

- 15 minutes per day at home earns you $100,000 per year
- Get flat abs in time for summer with 10 can't-miss weight loss secrets
- Shocking photos reveal: Obama is an Alien!

OK, I made that last one up, but you get the point.

Get the keywords right

Since you're writing for both your visitors and the search engines, keep in mind that you need to work your keywords into the headline. Search engines tend to give more weight to the keywords near the beginning of the headline, so try to get your keywords into the sentence as early as possible. Maybe our grocery store headlines should really read:

- **Work from home**: $100,000 per year in 15 minutes per day!

- **10 weight loss secrets**: Flat abs in time for summer!

- **Obama an Alien**? Shocking photos reveal the truth!

I've bolded the first few words to show you what the search engines will give the most credence to.

Be useful, create urgency, be unique

Of course, writing fantastical, tabloid headlines doesn't work for every site. Write headlines that grab your user's attention. Maybe if you were writing for the Drupal community, your headlines would read:

- 7 Drupal design secrets to accelerate your development!

- Drupal convention 2020 to be held on the South Pole!

- 10 Drupal Server speed tweaks you can do right now!

- morten.dk an Alien? Shocking photos reveal the truth!

 morten.dk is a top Drupal theme designer who lives in Copenhagen and organizes many Drupal events and post-event parties around the globe. Party on!

Now that you've got a great title, let's work on that body.

Good body content

Writing good body content is much harder than writing the headline. After all, it's 100 times longer! A typical page on a web site is 600 to 1,000 words long. That's about one single-spaced page in a Word doc. Much more than that and your visitor won't read it. Much less and they don't feel that there is enough substance to get their needs met. Of course there are exceptions to this, like your FAQ, but in general, you should stick to this guideline.

The base site pages

Base pages are the anchor content on any site and are always visible. They're considered the main pages and they don't change or move around much. These are the pages that you'll build links to and will probably show up in the search engines for the most difficult terms. The following are some good base pages on your site that you should consider creating. They're easy to create and are a positive addition to any site:

- Product Information
- About Us
- F.A.Q.
- Customer Testimonials
- Calendar of Upcoming Events
- Blog
- Employee Profiles
- Press Releases
- White Papers
- Step-by-Step solutions

Supplemental pages

Supplemental pages are the pages on your site that support your core pages. They're relevant, but wouldn't be considered the primary site message. They'll show up in the search engines for long-tail keywords. Long-tail keywords are keywords that are 3 or more words long and tend to be searched less often. But, they're still valuable to your site. They may be pages or stories, blog posts, or even user-generated content like forums.

What information would be interesting to your visitors that supplements your core content? Be creative. The goal is to be a trusted source that provides both education and entertainment to your visitors. Not only does this contribute to your natural SEO efforts, it provides value to your customers. You should build a solid content base, and continue to add to it regularly.

For example, if you sell Christmas trees, you could provide an ongoing series of articles. You can make use of the following titles:

- The History of Christmas trees
- How to decorate a tree
- How to recycle a Christmas tree
- Famous Christmas trees

Remember, your visitors are skimming, not reading. They'll stop and read only if they see something interesting. Therefore, make it easy for them to skim your content. Make use of the following techniques:

- Use the first sentence of each paragraph like a mini-headline to draw the reader's attention.
- Make use of bullets when making a list of things since they makes it easy to follow and draws the eye.
- Break up your content with sub-headlines. An <H2> tag would do the trick. Make logical breaks in the content, based on what you're writing about, in that section.
- Make use of bold key words or key ideas in the paragraphs.
- Throughout your written content, carefully sprinkle images that communicate your idea.

Another good way to draw your reader in is to give them options at the bottom of each content page. Maybe it's a call to action, "Buy our widget now!", or simply links to other, related content on your site.

Search engine optimizing content

Just creating the content isn't usually enough to get you top billing in the search engines. You'll need to tweak it to show up on the front page of Google.

Keywords

First things first, optimize your current content for keywords. Don't force it, but incorporate them into your text where it is appropriate. Adding a keyword once in the page title, once in the headline headline, and a couple of times in the body content should be enough.

Don't stuff keywords

A common misperception by site owners is that the more keywords they use, the better their ranking will be. Repeating keywords ad nauseum will be unnatural and is a major turn-off for both search engines and visitors. You've seen it before:

Our widget is the best widget of all the widgets because Widgetco widgets build superior widgets.

Ugh! Terrible stuff. Clearly, the goal is to get some Google love, not to communicate well with the visitors. Instead, write naturally, communicating to your visitors first. Adding in a keyword here and there shouldn't break good grammar.

Keyword density

Keyword density is the density of the keywords on a given page of your site. For example, if your keyword is **fast computer** and that phrase appears six times among the 200 words on the page then you have a 3% keyword density. There is not a hard and fast rule about the best keyword density for SEO. In fact, some people don't believe that it matters at all. However, it's a pretty good idea to at least pay attention and make sure that the keyword you want to rank for is showing up on your site at least three or four times.

Freshness

Google and other search engines will frequently scan your web site for new information. If your site is static, you are being ignored. Think of your web site as a work in progress, a database of information that is continually being added to. For example, you can write a few articles in a series, and post one each month, or you can create a News page that is updated frequently with company or industry news.

Optimizing category pages

Category pages are special kinds of pages on your site that take some careful consideration when doing SEO. When you think about categories, it's easy to see how they're powerful ways for visitors to see batches of your content. If you're on `http://www.amazon.com` (perhaps buying this book for all your friends) and you click on the **Business & Investing** category, all of the other books in the store are stripped away, leaving you with nothing but books that match your need at that moment. Click again on the **Marketing & Sales** category and you'll see books related to that topic. The other great thing about category pages is that they can be optimized to show up in Google for search terms that bring a lot of traffic to your site.

In Drupal, category pages can be generated by the built-in taxonomy module or the views module. Every time you add a tag or a category to a node, you're building a category page in Drupal that lists that node. By optimizing that page, you can get some great listings in Google. Earlier in this chapter, I showed you the best use of heading tags. Here are some additional best practices:

1. Go to `http://www.yourDrupalsite.com/admin/content/taxonomy/list` and click the **edit vocabulary** button. Enter a good, keyword-rich description into the **Description** field.

2. If there are some good sub-sections of this category, create a block that lists them. Make sure the block has keyword-rich anchor text on the links, and is set only to display when that category page is being viewed. You may even consider creating a simplified main navigation, or even hiding the main navigation on that category page.

Bold, strong, and emphasized text

Many search engines take into account text that is set apart on the page. You can set apart a word or phrase using a couple of methods. Bold and italics will do just that, bold or italicize the text. `<strong>` and `<em>` are terms that can be styled to look like anything you'd like using a style sheet in your theme. Typically, strong and emphasis tend to look like bold or italics. All are good methods for pulling a word out of a block of text and making it stand out.

	Tag	Looks like
Bold	`<b></b>`	**This text is bold.**
Strong	`<strong></strong>`	**This text is strong.**
Italics	`<i></i>`	*This text is italicized.*
Emphasis	`<em></em>`	*This text is emphasized.*

What to write about

Now that you know how to write and optimize the text on the page, what do you write about? If there is only one thing you take away from this chapter, it should be the following.

Write for your audience, not the search engines

For the long-term benefit of your site, you should create content that users will enjoy. Over time, this will give you the most SEO benefit. Beyond that, here are some guidelines:

- Use words that your audience understands. If you're writing for techies, use techie terms and don't apologize for them. If you're a techie company trying to attract non-techie customers, explain everything. Acronyms are the secret language of the clique. Only use them if you don't care if someone doesn't understand. However, you stand a good chance of alienating your audience if you do.

- Use words that will attract the right people to your site. Different words mean different things to people. Try to think like your target audience. If they're calling it a **Thingy** and you keep referring to **Widgets**, you're going to lose at least part of the people who visit. Also, the keywords you put into your site will be discovered by people looking for explanations. At least refer to a location where people can get their answers.

- Always keep Google in the back of your mind. I know, I know. I said not to worry about Google. However, do keep them in mind because they are one of the most important visitors to your site. Put your keywords in the right places and fill gaps in the search engines. Find areas in your industry that aren't covered well by others, or that have a very limited amount of good pages explaining them, and write about it.

Be timely

People are looking for insight into the world around them. What can you add to the news item that just came out on `http://www.CNN.com`? How can you tie your products and services into what's going on? It's easier than you think.

Google News Alerts

Set up a Google News Alert to email you whenever a news story comes out that's relevant to your business. This will give you a daily stream of ideas to write about. Carry out the following steps to receive email from Google News Alert whenever there's a news story:

1. Go to `http://news.Google.com/`.

2. Perform a search on a topic that you're interested in. It doesn't matter if there aren't any results yet. You should see a screen similar to the following screenshot:

3. Click on the **News Alerts** icon in the left column. You'll get to select some
    options regarding where and how you'd like to receive your news alerts:

4. Click on the **Create Alert** button.

5. If you selected that the alert be delivered via email, you will be sent an email
    confirming your Google News alert.

You can also add your alert to a Newsreader as RSS. This will deliver timely content
from many web sites that you can use as inspiration. We'll cover how to do that in
the upcoming section.

Newsreaders are your friends

A time-honored tradition among writers is to find out what other people are writing about and then borrow their ideas. Don't plagiarize, of course, but use other people's content as the launching point for your own creative process. If you do use a lot of their ideas, be sure to credit them. There are many great web sites out there that can provide you with great content to get the ball rolling, but it's time consuming to visit a bunch of web sites every day. Use RSS and a Newsreader to bring all of the content together in one place.

You know in those futuristic TV shows, where the newspaper is dynamic and writes itself based on what the particular reader wants? Well, the future is now and it's called RSS + Newsreaders. OK, maybe your paper newspaper is still the same as it ever was, but you can do something very similar with the right tools.

We talked about RSS feeds back in Chapter 7, *robots.txt, .htaccess, and W3C Validation*. Now, let's create a Google Newsreader account and set it up to show you great content from around the web by carrying out the following steps:

1. Go to `http://reader.google.com`. You should see a Google sign in screen that looks like the following screenshot:

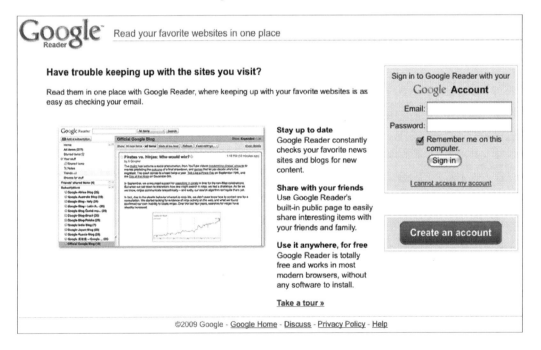

2. Log in using your Google account. This is the same account that you created in Chapter 1, *The Tools You'll Need*, to sign up for Google Analytics.

3. You should see a **Welcome to Google Reader!** screen, as shown in the following screenshot:

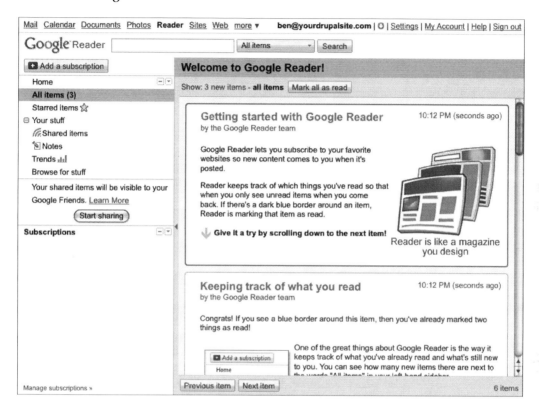

4. Now, let's add some good RSS feeds. We'll start with my Drupal SEO blog which can be found at `http://volacci.com/blog/ben-finklea`. On my page, you'll see an RSS icon, as shown in the following screenshot:

5. This is a typical indication on many blogs and web sites that there is an RSS feed for this content. If you click on that icon, many modern browsers will detect that it's an RSS feed and ask you if you would like to add it to your Google Reader account. Try it. If that works, you're done. If that doesn't work, proceed to step 6.

6. Right-click on the icon and copy the URL.

7. Go to the **Google Reader** screen and click the **Add a subscription** button, paste in the URL of the RSS feed, and click the **Add** button:

8. Now, you'll see all my recent blog posts, as shown in the following screenshot:

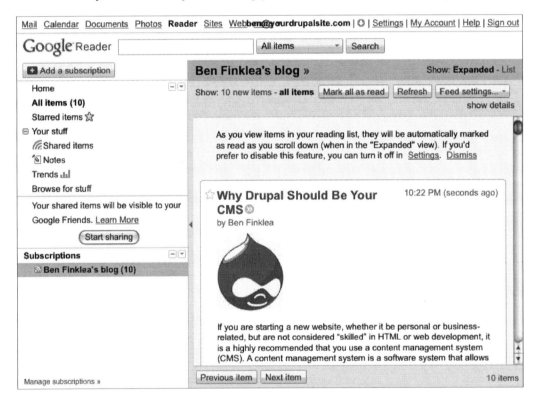

9. Repeat steps 4 to 7 for any sites that you like or are relevant to your industry.

If you need help finding good sources, try one of these:

- Google Blog Search: `http://blogsearch.google.com`
- Technorati: `http://technorati.com`
- Drupal Planet: `http://drupal.org/planet`
- NPR: `http://www.npr.org/rss/`
- About: `http://www.about.com/`

Now that you've got all your feeds set up, be sure to bookmark your Google Reader page and visit it daily or whenever you need inspiration.

Be yourself

Your parents always told you to be yourself, didn't they? Well, you finally get to do it. There are other people out there like you so why not do business with them? Build your personality into your writing and you'll be amazed at how it will resonate with others.

Write like you, y' know, talk

Writing can be tedious if you're trying to change your style to something that you're not. Instead, just write like you talk. If it comes into your head, then put it down. Change it if it just doesn't fit, but don't worry about it. Write like you're talking to your best friend. Write like you're talking to one person. Get them in your mind and then just launch into what you want them to hear.

Write what you know

If you want to sound credible, don't write on topics that you don't know about. Or, at least do some research so your readers will trust what you're saying. Since most of your content will be about what your site or company does, this shouldn't be too hard. With a well-researched article you can generate a lot of trust with your site visitors. Plus, it's OK if you don't know everything. Just admit that up front, so your users will give you the benefit of the doubt if you flub up the details. That's a great way to solicit feedback: 'Hey, I'm no Widget cleaner expert here. Let me know if I got this right...'

Build relationships

Another thing to remember when creating content for your site is that it's all to develop relationships with real people. They'll read your blog, they'll leave a comment, they'll bump into you at a tradeshow, and so on.

Talk about what other people are doing

One of the fastest ways to get other people to read your content is to write about them. See a cool project happening somewhere in your industry? Write about it. Then, email them and say, 'I wrote about you! Care to comment?'. Not only will they comment, there's a good chance they'll write about your post on their site. Tada! Instant new readers.

Interact early and often

If someone posts a comment, reply! Even if it's just with, 'Thanks for the comment!'. You're at least letting them know that you're paying attention and you appreciate their effort. If someone asks a question, reply to it with a good answer. If you can, send them an email with your reply since they may not visit the site again unless you do.

If you say something controversial, and it starts a firestorm, well, that's good! More readers! Just don't let someone say something bad about you without responding to it. A few months ago I posted an article about link building that, if read the wrong way, could imply that I was advocating comment spamming. No! That's a disaster and my readers said so. So, I quickly posted my clarification and thanked readers for their comments. Tough? Yes. Worth it? Absolutely. Learn from my mistakes and check it out at the following web site:

```
http://www.volacci.com/blog/ben-finklea/2009/may/01/researching-
backlinks-drupal-seo
```

Link to others

Writing great content will get you great links. A quick way to accelerate that is to link to other people in your blog posts. There are many blog services out there that will alert site owners when there is a new link to their site. Just by linking to other people, you'll see more traffic to your site when they come to see what you said. Say something nice and interesting and they're likely to talk about it and link back to you.

Don't stop

One of the biggest traffic-killers is to shut up. It can be discouraging in the early months of blogging or writing content when you've only got three people reading, and one of them is your mom. Hey, that's the way it is for everyone. Just keep writing great content. Publish your RSS feed far and wide. Interact with others. Your readership will slowly go up.

Find inspiration

Here's my inspiration list for writing blog posts. When I get stuck, I work down the following list until I find something I want to write about:

- Google News.
- Google Alerts.
- The Daily Beast.
- Print magazines
- TV.
- Radio.
- Other blogs.
- http:// www.Drupal.org.
- Drupal Planet.
- Emails you received.
- Questions a customer asked you.
- Recycle your old posts—write an update.
- Read through the comments on your previous posts.
- Examine the pros and cons of an issue, topic, update, upgrade, and so on.
- Interview people. People are busy but everyone wants to spread their ideas. As busy as I am, I have never turned down an interview request, ever.
- Books. Apply general ideas from books in a specific way that's relevant to your niche.
- Make a top 10, top 50, top 100 list. Then, over the course of several blog posts, write about each item on the list. Or, interview someone about each item.
- Use http:// www.search.twitter.com to find posts that are relevant to your business. Write about what other people are talking about.
- Write a joke post making fun of, well, anything.
- Do some original research. This is great for link bait!

- Debunk a myth.
- Write a how-to for beginners in your industry.
- Write a funny story about how you first found out about your industry.
- Write about what you learned at a tradeshow.
- Create a best-of list of great blog posts from that day.
- Write an FAQ for your niche.
- Blog about an event as it happens.

Do a week at a time

If you're busy, and you're writing a blog a day, it can be tedious to find the necessary time. Instead, write a week's worth of posts at one time, and then use the Scheduler module to post one blog each day. The Scheduler module is maintained by Eric Schaefer. Schedule time to thank Eric when you get a chance.

Carry out the following steps to set up the Scheduler module:

1. Download the Scheduler module from the following link, `http://drupal.org/project/scheduler` and install it just like a normal Drupal module. Refer to Chapter 1, *The Tools You'll Need*, for step-by-step module installation instructions.

2. Go to `http://www.yourDrupalsite.com/admin/settings/scheduler`, or go to your admin screen and click on **Administer | Site configuration | Scheduler module settings** link. You'll see a screen similar to the following screenshot:

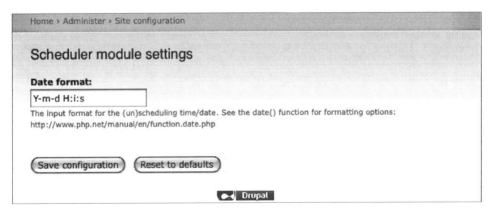

Leave this alone for now.

3. Go to `http://www.yourDrupalsite.com/admin/content/types` or go to your admin screen and click the **Administer | Content management | Content Types** link and click on **edit** option, located next to the type of content that you would like to schedule.

4. Open the **Workflow settings** drop-down. You will see a screen similar to the following screenshot:

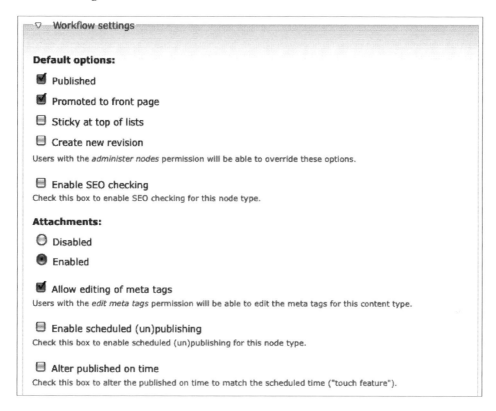

5. Select the **Enable scheduled (un)publishing** and the **Alter published on time** checkboxes. The former will allow scheduling on this content type and the latter will change the date of the post that your readers see to match the date you scheduled the post to appear. Generally, this is a good idea.

6. Click on **Save content type**.

   Now, when you create a new post, you'll have an additional option called **Scheduling options**.

▽ Scheduling options

Publish on:

Format: *2009-05-25 06:12:28*. Leave blank to disable scheduled publishing.

Unpublish on:

Format: *2009-05-25 06:12:28*. Leave blank to disable scheduled unpublishing.

---

7. Enter the date that you would like the post to appear in the **Publish on** field. If you want it to show up immediately, then you can leave it blank. Also, if your post is something that is only appropriate for a certain amount of time (like a sale, or a calendar event), then enter an **Unpublish on** time as well.

8. Click on **Save**.

9. Check to see that it's working properly. If it's not working, make sure that you've properly set up cron to run on a regular basis.

Scheduling your posts saves a lot of time and helps to keep things fresh on your site.

Using Drupal to organize your content

Drupal is not just a way to easily manage large amounts of content, it actually helps you keep that content organized and structured as well. This is a terrific asset to your SEO campaign. Search engines want to know what your site is all about: primary topics, subtopics, related headings, and so on, all help. By using the built-in Drupal tools, your site can be in top shape for the search engines.

Structure your site hierarchically

There's a reason you learned the outlining format in grade school. It's easier to organize related ideas when they're structured hierarchically. It turns out that it's easier for search engines to figure your site out when it's structured that way as well. So, send a long-overdue thank you note to your fifth grade language arts teacher and let's get organized.

It keeps things organized

Organized content is useful content. Keep similar ideas together and your site will be more useful to your visitors. It's also easy to see where you might have a weakness in your site's content. If you've got five pages on topics A and B, but only one page on topic C, then you know where to focus your writing efforts. Finally, Drupal allows you to create RSS feeds around any topic. That makes it easy for visitors who are interested in new widgets to keep track of your R&D department while avoiding the content about your cat's latest misadventure in the garbage disposal.

Google likes it better

Search engines also need to work in an organized manner. It turns out that search engines organize around much broader concepts than just keywords (although keywords are still the most important element). To find related words that will help your ranking, try typing your keyword into Google, in the following manner:

~yourkeyword

This is an approximate, or synonym, search. It finds terms that are related to the one you're searching for. Pay attention to the bolded items in the search results and you'll see keywords that Google considers approximate and relevant. Write content around those terms and Google will rank you higher. This is true even if the original term didn't show up in your content.

It's easier to build keywords into your categories

If you have great categories and loads of content in those categories, it's easy to add a few relevant keywords to the category pages. If your content is spread out over too many categories, or it's not organized at all, it's almost impossible to get all those ideas onto one page.

Siloing

There's a fancy word going around in SEO circles called **Siloing**. It's the concept of building your site around a series of concepts that are all related to your primary site topic. Basically, you build different sections of your site on subtopics that all support the main idea. In other words, build your site hierarchically and organized around categories. It turns out that Drupal's built in modules do this for you already, which is another reason that Drupal is the best platform for SEO.

Using taxonomy to organize around the main topics

For the main content of your site, you should create a taxonomy category with a handful of keyword-rich terms that all of your content will fit under. Do not allow free tagging in this main content category as it creates too many categories and becomes a nightmare to maintain. If you want to have free tagging for other types of content, like blogs or products, (and it's a good idea in many cases) then create a separate taxonomy for it.

Don't go crazy with deep hierarchies. It makes sense in some cases, but a good rule of thumb is that no content should be more than three clicks from the home page. Obviously this doesn't apply if you have 10,000 pages, but for most sites, this is very easy to achieve with a good directory structure. The closer the node is to the home page, the more important Google thinks it is, and the higher that individual page will rank (remember, this is a rule of thumb, not a hard and fast rule so don't destroy your site's usability to make this happen).

Creating structured URL paths

Using Drupal, it's easy to build the illusion of structure into the paths. You can easily set up the Path module to create paths that look like the following URL:

```
http://yourDrupalsite.com/products/fastcars/bens-ferrari.htm
```

When the content really exists at `/?q=node/123`. This can be very helpful for your organization if you set up a category page at `/products` and `/products/fastcars`. This gives your site a nice, clean hierarchical structure, making it easier for visitors to find their way around.

Removing content

Not all content is good content. There will come a time when you want to take something off of your site. If you want to be friendly with the search engines, don't just unpublish the node. Search engines are crawling through your site on a regular basis and assigning value to each page. If you delete a page, you're just throwing that value away which is a loss for your site.

Take the time to do it right and you can redirect all of the search engine goodness that your page carries to another page on your site, or even to another web site entirely.

Here's a quick checklist for deleting or moving a piece of content. Before removing the node or page:

1. Decide which existing page on your site will catch all of the traffic that used to go to the page you're deleting. Or, you may need to create one. This page should be in some way relevant to the old page.

2. Remove or update all links to the page that appear on your site. Visitors will find those broken links and get frustrated if you don't update them.

3. Do a backlink search using Google Webmaster Tools, by carrying out the following steps:

    °   Log in to Google Webmaster Tools.
    °   Click on the domain you're working with. You'll see the Dashboard, scroll down to the **Links to your site** section and click on the **More** button.
    °   Click on the number, located next to the page you're removing, and you'll see a list of the sites linking to that page.

4. Email everyone linking to that page letting them know that the page is moving, and ask them to update their link to point to the new page.

5. Set up a 301 redirect using the Path redirect module.

6. Test the 301 redirect.

Summary

Content is king! With great content comes a great result in your SEO campaign, along with a high satisfaction and conversion rate for your visitors. There are many ways to organize your content, each with its pros and cons. The key is to find the topics that are relevant to your site and stick with them.

In this chapter, we have covered the following topics:

*   Good Content
*   How to Write for Your Audience
*   How to SEO your Content
*   What to Write About
*   Organizing Content
*   Removing Content

In the next chapter, we'll see some cool ways to use Calais to automatically organize content and discuss how to prevent Spam.

9
Taking Control of Your Content

It's time to take control of your content. How your site is organized, and how all of the content links together, is very important to your standing with the search engines. Making sure your content is well structured and doesn't violate any HTML best practices, is another way to show that your site is the best. Also, making sure there aren't links on your site to bad neighborhoods (gambling, porn, Viagra, hate, and so on) will ensure that you aren't penalized in the search engines results. In this chapter, we will cover the following topics:

- Using OpenCalais to tag and organize your content
- Bulk processing your content with OpenCalais
- Creating **More Like This** blocks to help visitors and the search engines know more about your site
- Keeping your content compliant with the HTML Purifier module
- Blocking spam with the Mollom module

Using OpenCalais to tag and organize your content

Suppose you've got hundreds of pages of content on your site and you haven't been doing a very good job so far of categorizing everything. Or, perhaps you have a lot of users creating posts every day, and it's too much trouble to train everyone or go back through and tag everything that's created. Well, there's an automated solution called **OpenCalais** (also known as Calais) that will do the heavy lifting for you.

- OpenCalais reads in the content of your nodes, as you create them, or in bulk
- OpenCalais uses some amazing analysis to create tags for your content
- OpenCalais creates tags in your Drupal Taxonomies so you can use them to organize your content

OpenCalais is not perfect. It only tags three major types of data:

1. **Named entities**: People, companies, organization, geographies, books, albums, authors, and so on.
2. **Facts**: Position, alliance, person-education, person-political, and so on.
3. **Events**: Sporting, management change, IPO, labor action, and so on.

If your content doesn't discuss this kind of data very often, then OpenCalais may not be for you. To find out, try out their Document Viewer at the following link:

```
http://viewer.opencalais.com/
```

Introducing the Symantic Web

OpenCalais is part of a new revolution on the web called **Symantic Web**. The idea is that all content of the web can be structured in such a way that computers can talk to each other easily and carry out transactions on our behalf without human involvement. Wouldn't it be cool if you could tell your computer you have a toothache and it would create a convenient appointment time at your local dentist, place that appointment on your calendar, get approval from your HMO, and send driving instructions to your phone the day of the appointment? The Symantic Web is a step in that direction.

In 1999, Tim Berners-Lee, the founder of the World Wide Web said, 'I have a dream for the Web in which computers become capable of analyzing all the data on the Web—the content, links, and transactions between people and computers. A Semantic Web, which should make this possible, has yet to emerge, but when it does, the day-to-day mechanisms of trade, bureaucracy and our daily lives will be handled by machines talking to machines. The **intelligent agents** people have touted for ages will finally materialize.'

A special thanks to the OpenCalais team for taking the time to field about 50 questions I had during their DrupalCon DC 2009 presentation. Also, thanks to Angie Byron (also known as WebChick) for writing up a good primer on OpenCalais at `http://www.lullabot.com/articles/introduction-calais`. When she's not writing up fantastic walkthroughs, Angie is the Drupal 7 core maintainer. Thanks for all you do, Angie! Where do you find the time?

Installing OpenCalais on your Drupal site

It takes two different modules and an extra download to get OpenCalais working. It's not difficult, though. Just carry out the following steps:

1. Firstly, install the modules by carrying out the following steps:
   ○ Download the **Resource Description Framework (RDF)** module from `http://www.drupal.org/project/rdf` and install it just like a normal Drupal module. See Chapter 1 for step-by-step module installation instructions. However, do not enable it until you've finished Step 2 and have installed ARC 2 RDF classes for PHP.
   ○ Download the OpenCalais module from `http://www.drupal.org/project/opencalais` and install it just like a normal Drupal module. See Chapter 1 for step-by-step module installation instructions. When you turn the module on, be sure to turn on both Calais and Calais API.

2. Download ARC 2 RDF classes for PHP from the following link, `http://arc.semsol.org/download` and install into the RDF module's `vendor` folder. You'll need to create the vendor folder here: `sites/all/modules/rdf/vendor/`.

3. Enable the RDF module on the modules page.

4. Get an OpenCalais API key. An API key gives you access to their services using a Drupal module. It's a simple, two-step process that takes about three minutes. You'll create an account, and then request the API key. It all starts at the following link: `http://www.opencalais.com/GetStarted`.

5. Go to `http://www.yourDrupalsite.com/admin/settings/calais`, or go to your admin screen and click the **Administer | Site Configuration | Calais Configuration** link. You'll see a screen similar to the following screenshot:

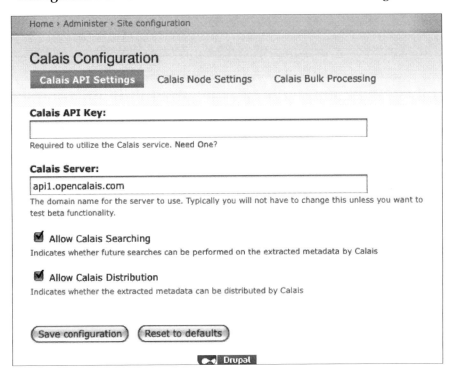

6. Paste in your Calais API key and click on **Save configuration**.

7. Next, click the **Calais Node Settings** tab.

8. Configure your settings as follows:

   ○ **Store Calais RDF Locally**: Leave it checked.

   ○ **Global**: This is a list of all of the types of content that OpenCalais knows about. Unless you're experiencing a problem, you should leave all of these checked.

   ○ **Blog entry**, **Page**, **Story**: These are the content types that are currently enabled on your site. You can configure OpenCalais to only run on the content types that you want.

- ° **Calais Processing**: This determines how the terms that Calais returns to your site will be used. Suggesting all of the ways to automatically applying them. For SEO purposes, choose **Apply all suggested terms on every update**. However, to start out, you might want to choose **Suggest terms, but DON'T apply them** so that you can see what it's doing and offer your own suggestions making OpenCalais work better. Cool!

- ° **Allow Calais Searching**: This option allows OpenCalais to search your metadata in the future. This makes their service work better so leave this checked.

- ° **Allow Calais Distribution**: This option gives OpenCalais permission to distribute your metadata to other sites. This is a good thing that could result in other sites linking to your or sending traffic your way. Leave this checked.

- ° **Relevancy Threshold**: OpenCalais may not be 100% sure about the tags that it produces. This setting allows you to tell it how sure it must be before it applies the tags to your site. A setting of 0.00 will apply every tag no matter what and a setting of 1.00 will only apply tags that it's very sure about. You can put anything in between. Start out with a setting of 0.50 and adjust as necessary.

- ° **Use Calais Global Entity defaults**: This uses the built-in categories that OpenCalais defines. Leave this checked.

9. Click on **Save configuration**.

10. Now, create a node. I grabbed a post from Wikipedia about Barak Obama and pasted it into a story node. Notice that there is a newly created tab called **Calais**. Click that tab. You should see a screen similar to the following screenshot:

11. Since we asked OpenCalais to not tag automatically, it only makes suggestions. If you like what you see, you can copy and paste the suggestions into the boxes provided. You can also turn on automatic tagging and the OpenCalais module will do it for you. With tagging turned on, it looks like the following screenshot:

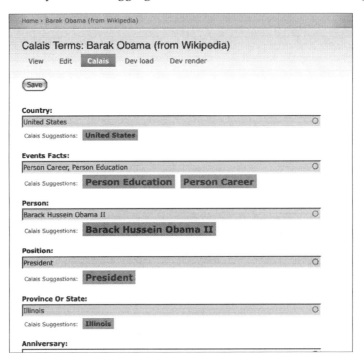

Now take a look at your **Taxonomy** list by pointing your browser to the following link, `http://www.yourDrupalsite.com/admin/content/taxonomy/list`. You'll see a list of all of the OpenCalais categories. Any node that is processed by OpenCalais that has a term in one of those categories will create the terms. For example, click on the taxonomy **Person** after you've passed the President Obama node through it and you'll see a screen similar to the following screenshot:

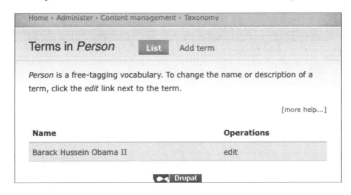

Very cool! Now any story you post that talks about President Obama will be categorized in this term which makes for easy and instant organization.

Using OpenCalais' bulk processing to tag existing content

Maybe you've got a site with a lot of content already. Consider using OpenCalais' Bulk Processing to go through your site and create tags for each piece of content. This is a very quick way to organize your content, you just need to carry out the following steps:

1. After you have OpenCalais installed on your Drupal site, point your browser to `http://www.yourDrupalsite.com/admin/settings/calais/bulk-process`, or navigate to **Administer | Site configuration | Calais Configuration | Calais Bulk Processing**. You'll see a screen similar to the following screenshot:

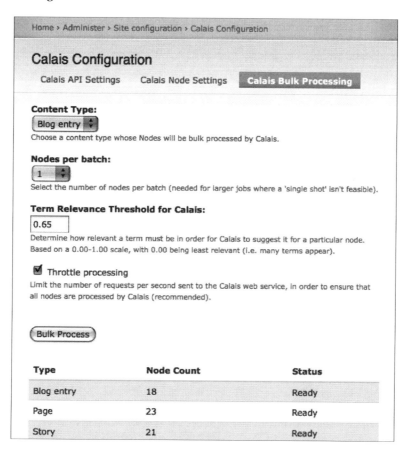

2. The settings are straightforward. Select the **Content Type**, **Nodes per batch**, **Term Relevance Threshold for Calais**, and **Throttle processing** and then click **Bulk Process**.

3. You should see a success message, as shown in the following screenshot:

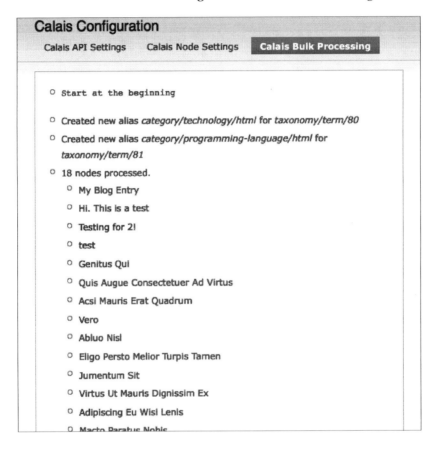

Now that all your content has been processed by OpenCalais, there are many things you can do with your content that wasn't available to you before, like **More Like This** blocks and RDF.

Using OpenCalais to offer 'More Like This' blocks

One of the ways that search engines determines the relevance of a piece of content to a particular topic is where it links to and which pages link to it. For example, real estate and mortgages are related to Google because a lot of realtors link to mortgage companies and vice versa.

A **More Like This** block shows your visitors more content that is similar to what is being displayed on the page. This is not only good to increase the amount of time visitors spend on your site, but it's also a great way to tell Google what content is related.

1. Make sure you have OpenCalais properly installed.

2. Download the **More Like This** module from `http://www.drupal.org/` `project/morelikethis` and install just like a normal Drupal module. Refer to Chapter 1, *The Tools You'll Need*, for step-by-step module installation instructions.

    ○   When activating the module, turn on both the **More Like This** module and the MLT—Taxonomy module.

    ○   Note that the **More Like This** module is dependent on the Autoload module which you can download from `http://www.drupal.org/project/autoload`.

3. Go to `http://www.yourDrupalsite.com/admin/settings/morelikethis`, or go to your admin screen and click the **Administer | Site configuration | More Like This Settings** link. You'll see a screen similar to the following screenshot:

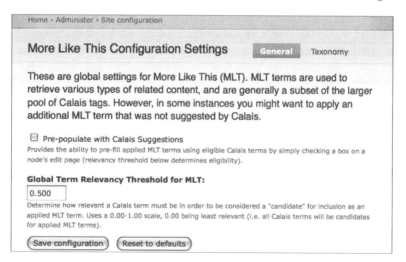

4. Note that there are two tabs of settings, **General** and **Taxonomy**.

5. The General settings are straightforward. Make sure **Pre-populate with Calais Suggestions** is selected and leave the **Global Term Relevancy Threshold for MLT** set at **0.500**. (You can experiment with the threshold on your site until its perfect.) Note that the **Relevancy Threshold** determines how close another piece of content must be to the node in question. If you're not getting any relevant content, try lowering this number.

6. Click on **Save configuration**.

7. Under the Taxonomy tab you can enable all of the content types that you wish to display a **More Like This** block on each node and set up how it will work. Open the Content type you wish to enable with **More Like This** and edit the settings, as shown in the following screenshot:

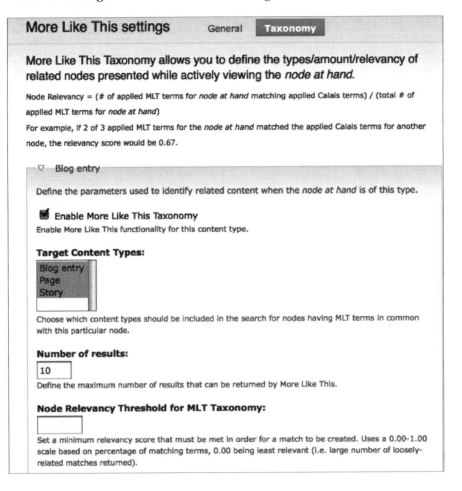

-   ◦ Select the **Enable More Like This Taxonomy** checkbox to turn the More Like This functionality on.

-   ◦ Under **Target Content Types**, you're selecting the Content types, which the More Like This will search to find other modules that are relevant. For example, if you have the block turned on for your **Story** content type, do you want links to relevant blog content to show up in that block? If so, select Blog entry. You can select more than one type

- ° **Number of results** is the maximum number of related entries that **More Like This** will return.

- ° **Node Relevancy Threshold for MLT Taxonomy** is an override for the same setting on the **General** tab. Set it to a particular score if you need to override the setting for this particular Content type.

- ° Repeat these steps for each Content type you wish to enable.

8. Click on **Save configuration**.

9. Go to `http://www.yourDrupalsite.com/admin/build/block`, or **Administer | Site Building | Blocks** and move the **More Like This Taxonomy Block** into a Region that is visible to your users.

10. Click on the **Save blocks** option.

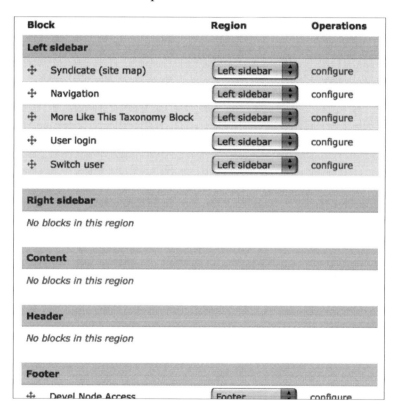

11. While still on the **Blocks** page, click on the **configure** option, located next to the **More Like This Taxonomy Block** and give it a more descriptive name like **More Cool Content You Might Like**.

12. Now, create a new piece of content that has More Like This enabled. You should see a section in the node creation screen that looks similar to the following screenshot:

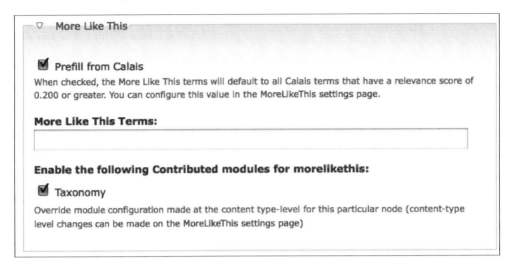

13. You can manually create associations by entering them in the **More Like This Terms** field, or you can just leave blank and OpenCalais will do the matching for you.

14. Click on **Save**.

15. If there is any content that is related to the node you just saved, you will see the More Like This block, as shown in the following screenshot:

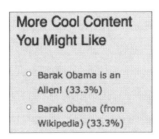

Your content is now more connected and that's a good thing for your site visitors and search engines.

But wait! That's not all you can do with OpenCalais!

There are even more cool things you can do now that you have OpenCalais installed. Try the following activities:

- Use Calais Marmoset to mark up your content with RDF Microformats.
- Use OpenCalais's Views module integration to create custom node lists based on Calais terms. For example, if you have a sports news web site, you could create a page for each team and player.
- Get your mashup on! Use the OpenCalais Geo module (built-in when you install Calais) to Geo-tag your content based on country, city, etc. Then, integrate your content into a Google map using the Gmap module.
- Use the Topic Hubs module to create customizable topic hubs based on Calais tags. A topic hub uses tagging rules that you specify to display groups of nodes.
- Basically, any module that gives you control over Taxonomies can (in theory) be used with Calais.

Keeping content compliant with the HTML Purifier module

Suppose you've run the W3C check and there are some problems with user-created content (You'd never make mistakes, would you?). You can easily fix it by editing the node, but how do you keep more issues from cropping up over time? The answer is the **HTML Purifier** module. This module utilizes a program called HTML Purifier that does several things to keep your code clean. It will:

- Remove malicious code with a secure yet permissive whitelist
- Make sure your documents are standards compliant

The HTML Purifier module is maintained by Edward Z. Yang. Thanks!

Carry out the following steps to install and configure it:

1. Download the HTML Purifier module from the following link, http://www.drupal.org/project/htmlpurifier and install just like a normal Drupal module, but don't activate it yet. Refer to Chapter 1, *The Tools You'll Need*, for step-by-step module installation instructions.

2. Download the HTML Purifier module from http://www.htmlpurifier.org/. You will need version 3.1.0RC1 or later. Extract it.

3. Move just the `library` folder from the HTML Purifier to the `sites/all/modules/htmlpurifier` directory.

4. Now go to **Administer | Site building | Modules** and activate the **HTML Purifier** module.

5. You now need to add the filter to your existing input formats.
    Point your browser to `http://www.yourDrupalsite.com/admin/settings/filters`, or go to your admin screen and click on **Administer | Site Configuration | Input Formats** link. You'll see something similar to the following screenshot:

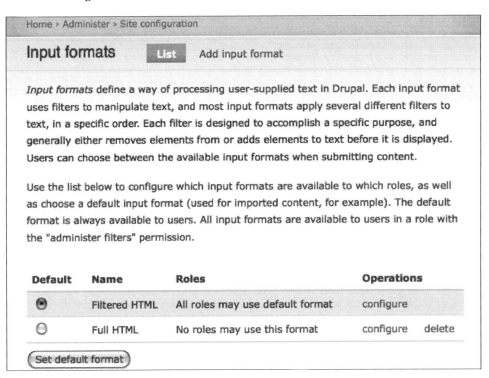

6. Click on the **configure** link next to **Filtered HTML** and you'll be able to see a screen similar to the following screenshot:

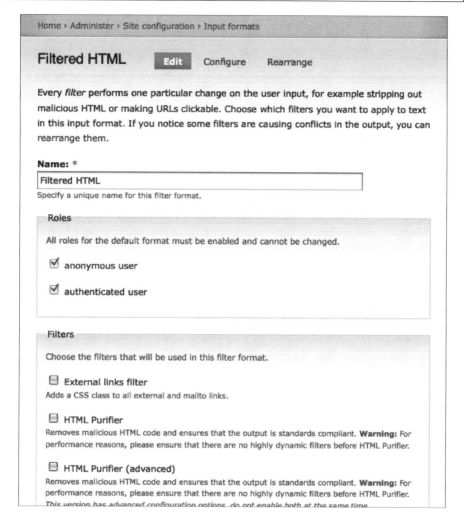

7. Select the **HTML Purifier** checkbox and then click on the **Save configuration** option.

8. Repeat the steps from 5 through 7 for each input format.

9. Test it! Create a node and put the following piece of code in the **Body** field and lick on **Save**:

```
<img src="javascript:evil();" onload="evil();" />
```

    View the source and you'll see that the evil JavaScript has been removed.

Now your site will stay compliant, even when people post bad code to your site.

Preventing spam

User comments are some of the best content that you have on your site as far as the search engines are concerned. They reinforce the ideas already on the page and the best thing of all is that you didn't need to lift a finger for someone to add value to your web site.

However, user comments introduce a whole set of problems called Comment Spam. Just because you have a web site, some users will use it as their own little playground for creating links back to anywhere they want. Fortunately, there is a terrific, and mostly automatic, service for preventing spam called **Mollom**. Mollom was created by Benjamin Schrauwen and Dries Buytuart (Recognize that name? He's the founder of Drupal!). Thanks guys, you've got a winner here!

Mollom is a web service that identifies comment quality and helps stop spam on your Drupal web site. Drupal web sites using Mollom send form submissions (comments, posts, and so on) that they want checked to http://www.mollom.com. Mollom then replies with either a spam or not-spam alert. If Mollom isn't sure, it will automatically ask the Mollom module to show a CAPTCHA challenge to the user, as shown in the following screenshot:

The coolest part is that sites can report or comment spam that Mollom missed. Mollom uses this information to adjust their algorithm and prevent future spam. This works pretty well as, according to `http://www.Mollom.com`, they're 99.96% effective at identifying spam. That comes to four misses for every 10,000 spam submissions. Pretty darn good!

Mollom pricing

Mollom offers a free version that does the trick for most web sites. However, if you have more than 100 legitimate comments per day, you'll need the paid version of Mollom. At the time of this writing, the paid service starts at about $50 per month. Find out more at `http://www.Mollom.com`. If you need other options, consider the Spam module, AntiSpam module, and the reCAPTCHA module.

Installing Mollom

Like OpenCalais, Mollom is a module and a service. It's easy to install, though. Just carry out the following steps:

1. Download the Mollom module from `http://www.drupal.org/project/mollom` and install it just like a normal Drupal module. Refer to Chapter 1, *The Tools You'll Need,* for step-by-step module installation instructions.

2. Go to `http://www.mollom.com/user/register` and set up a new account (if you already have a Mollom account, skip this step). It's a Drupal site so it's straightforward. They'll send you an email for verification.

3. After you're logged in to `http://www.Mollom.com`, click on the **Manage sites** link in the upper-right hand corner. Then, click on the **Add new site** button.

4. Select the plan that is appropriate for your site. If you're not sure, start with **Mollom Free**, by clicking on the **Get Mollom Free** button.

5. Enter your URL and other necessary information. Complete your subscription by clicking on the **Complete your subscription** button.

6. You'll now see your site listed. Click the **view keys** link. Leave this page open as you'll need to come back to it in a few minutes.

7. Visit `http://www.yourDrupalsite.com/admin/settings/mollom`, or go to your admin screen and click on **Site configuration | Mollom** link. You'll see a screen similar to the following screenshot:

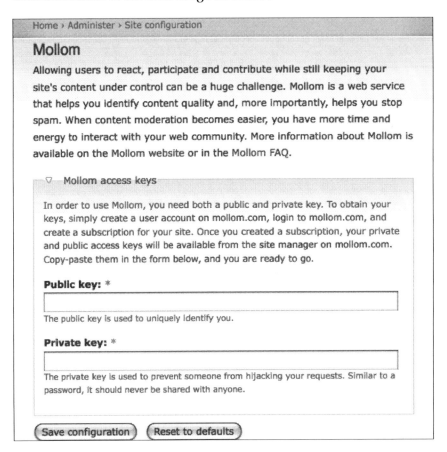

8. Copy and paste the **Public key** and **Private keys** from `http://www.Mollom.com` into the fields provided. Click on **Save configuration**. You'll see a confidence-inspiring message, as shown in the following screenshot:

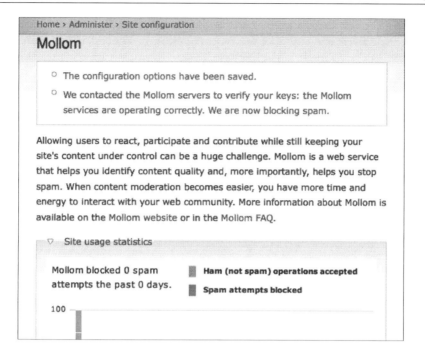

9. Scroll further down the page and you'll see several configuration options:

    ◦   **Protect comment form** is the option that protects you from comment spam. The standard setting of **Text analysis and CAPTCHA backup** should work well.

    ◦   **Protect user registration form** will protect you from spammer bots automatically creating user accounts. This should be set to **CAPTCHA only**.

    ◦   **Protect user password request form** keeps spambots from trying to guess easy user passwords on your site. This should be set to **CAPTCHA only**.

    ◦   The rest of the options will vary depending on which content types you have turned on in **Admin | Content Management | Content Types**. If you make certain node types available to public users, then set this option to **Text analysis and CAPTCHA backup**. However, if only employees or site admins can create content, then you might want to set to **No protection**. Keep an eye on things to make sure it's not being abused, though.

○ Under **Server settings**, you can set a **Fallback strategy**. This is critical for sites that are using Mollom's free service as there is no guarantee of uptime. Although, in my experience, Mollom is very reliable you should make a decision about what you want to happen if their servers go down. If in doubt, set this to **Block all submissions of protected forms until the server problems are resolved**. This will prevent any comments or content (including legitimate ones) until the Mollom server comes back online. If you have a site with a lot of users, you might consider leaving your site unprotected but be prepared for a deluge of Spam!

10. Click on **Save configuration**.

11. You should test this by submitting a comment to one of your sites. If you want to trigger Mollom, use words like Viagra and Nigeria. You should see something like this:

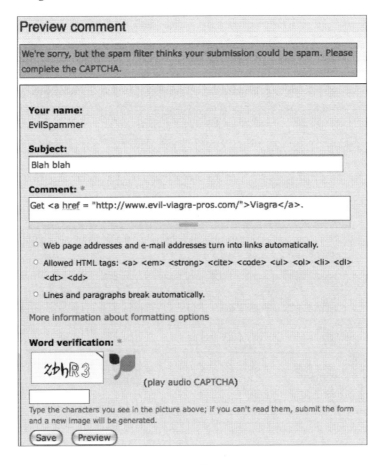

Now your site is being protected from the evil spam empire! You should consider going into **Administer | Content management** and updating the default settings on your content types to have Comments turned on.

Monitoring comments

Even with a proactive spam-protection service, you still need to be vigilant about spam. Mollom's pretty good but it's not perfect, and an occasional Spam will show up on your site. Here are some things you can do to help you monitor comments for Spam.

Using the Notify module

Use the Notify module to alert you whenever new content is posted to your site. You will not be notified of spam that was caught by Mollom. Glance through the rest to make sure they're all legitimate.

Giving Mollom feedback

When you do see Spam that slipped through the Mollom net, give them feedback. They've made it dead simple to delete spam and give them feedback all at one time. Here's how to report spam to Mollom:

1. Log in to your site as an admin.

2. When you see a comment on your site, you'll also see a **mark as abuse** link, as shown in the following screenshot:

I Spam you with Viagra!   Sun, 06/07/2009 - 17:30 — EvilSpammer

I am a Nigerian Prince! I want to give you free money!

delete   edit   reply   mark as abuse

3. If it's spam, click on the **mark as abuse** option. Then, you'll see many more options, as shown in the following screenshot:

Are you sure you want to delete the comment and report it?

Optionally report this to Mollom:

◉ Don't send feedback to Mollom

○ Report as spam or unsolicited advertising

○ Report as obscene, violent or profane content

○ Report as low-quality content or writing

○ Report as unwanted, taunting or off-topic content

Mollom is a web service that helps you moderate your site's content: see http://mollom.com for more information. By sending feedback to Mollom, you teach Mollom about the content you like and dislike, allowing Mollom to do a better job helping you moderate your site's content. If you want to report multiple posts at once, you can use Mollom's bulk operations on the content and comment administration pages.

This action cannot be undone.

(Delete) Cancel

---

4. Select the option that applies and click on **Delete**. Poof! The spam is gone.

Now you're bringing the anti-spam thunder.

Summary

Remember, you are in charge when it comes to the content on your Drupal site. That means that you should be leveraging every bit of content on your site to the fullest while protecting your valuable site assets from the bad guys.

In this chapter, we have covered:

- Using OpenCalais to tag and organize your content
- Bulk processing your content with OpenCalais
- Creating **More Like This** blocks to help visitors and the search engines know more about your site
- Keeping your content compliant with the HTML Purifier module
- Blocking spam with the Mollom module

Great content will get people to your site and even keep them there. But will they do what you want them to? The next chapter is all about increasing your conversion rate.

10

Increasing the Conversion Rate of Your Drupal Web site

One of the most overlooked areas of SEO is conversions. Many people talk about the virtues of being ranked at the top of Google but ultimately, they miss the primary goal of a typical business web site—to get those visitors to do what you want them to do. You should not think that conversion rates are just for e-commerce sites; all web sites have visitor conversion goals that can be measured, managed, and increased. In this final chapter, we're going to explore:

- The three main types of web sites and their conversion goals
- The common paths to conversions
- Incorporating strong calls to action to increase conversions
- Which analytics you should be paying attention to and which you should ignore
- Usability testing
- A/B testing with the Google Website Optimizer

What do you want them to do

Conversions mean different things to different web sites. The common conversion goals are stated in the following table:

Type of site	Primary Goal	Secondary Goal	Tertiary Goal
Lead generation	Fill out lead form	Send us email	Call us
e-commerce	Buy	Add to wish list	Sign up for newsletter
Ad-driven	Click more pages	Join	Subscribe to RSS feed

Your site goals may vary, so take some time to decide what you want your site's visitors to do. Are there other people in your organization who have a stake in the web site? Get their input and come up with a list of desired actions. Ask the following questions:

- How do people find your web site?

- How do you get customers?

- What do you want people to do on your site that makes your company money?

- What information is critical to the success of your sales efforts?

- Who are our most valuable customers?

- Who are our most regular customers? Do we want more of those?

- Are there particular products or services that we're trying to sell more of right now or in the near future?

- Are there customer service objectives for our web site or only sales objectives?

- What audiences (investors, employees, technical support, news media, and so on), besides customers, use our web site?

These are all considerations when making conversion decisions.

Path to conversion

Once you know what you want visitors to do, it's time to define clear steps you want them to take to do those things. The fantastic usability book, titled *Don't Make Me Think*, espouses the idea that it's not how many clicks someone has to go through; it's how easy it is to make the click decision. If clicking is easy and provides value then there's a high chance the user will take the next step towards becoming your customer.

Key to understanding what your customers are thinking is to understand what path they will take through your site. What follows are some simplified paths based on the type of web site. Using your analytics, write the percentage of people that take each action next to the decision point. Then, start working on the pages that have the worst results.

The following flowchart shows the process of e-commerce path to conversion:

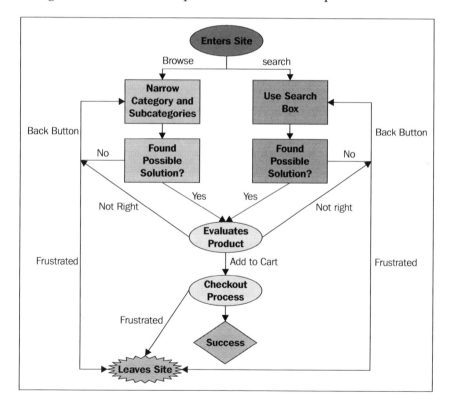

The following flowchart shows the process of lead generation paths to conversion:

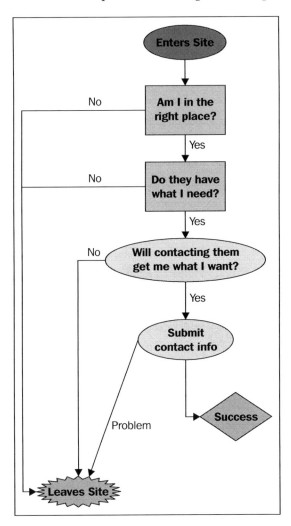

The following flowchart shows the process of ad-driven path to conversion:

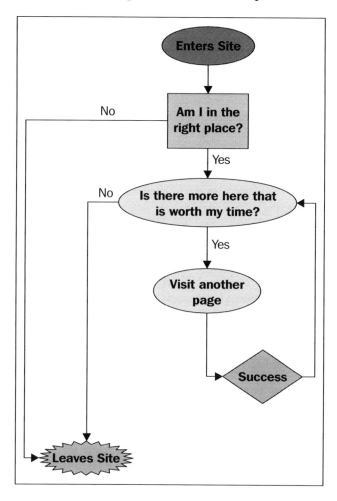

Strong calls to action

Once you know what you want them to do when they visit your site, you need to ask your visitors to do what you want them to do! No, I don't advocate actually coming right out and saying it but you should at least make it obvious and easy for them.

Phone number

One of the most obvious mistakes I see is from companies who want site visitors to call them. If you want people to call you, put your phone number big and in bold text at the top of every page. It's one of the easiest ways to tell people, 'Hey! Call us!'

Add to cart

For e-commerce sites, the ubiquitous **Add to Cart** button has become almost invisible to web visitors. What can you do to make it stand out? Try different colors and sizes, perhaps even flashing it once when the page is loading just to get the eyeballs to notice that there is an action to take. However you do it, make sure the **Add to Cart** button gets at least some of your attention.

Contact Us

Another great call to action is the **Contact Us** link. Just like the phone number, it should be prominent and easy to identify—not tacked on as an afterthought to the bottom of the page. Make sure the contact form is short, sweet, and only asks for information that you absolutely need to have—such as, name and phone number. Be sure to have an open field where people can type their own message to you. Give assurances as to how the information will be used and build trust by only using it that way.

Get a free white paper, watch a demonstration, or download a trial copy

This is a very effective method of building a house list—that internal list of email addresses that you can mine for customers. Giving something away is the tried and true marketing technique that continues to work. The key is to drive interested customers right to the freebie that they'd be most interested in.

Analytics to watch

The mantra of a great web site team should be 'measure everything'. We covered installing Google Analytics in Chapter 1, *The Tools You'll Need*. Understanding what and why you're tracking certain things will help you make sound design improvements to your web site. Not all data is useful, though. The analytics you should be paying attention to will vary by the type of web site that you run. Here's a quick classification of a few analytics:

	e-commerce	Lead Generation	Ad-Driven
Total Revenue	Critical	Critical	Critical
Total Profit	Critical	Critical	Critical
Profit Per Order	Critical	Critical	Not Important
Profit Margin	Critical	Good	Not Important
Conversions	Critical	Critical	Not Important
Conversion Rate	Critical	Critical	Not Important
Average Cost Per Conversion	Critical	Good	Not Important
Number of Visitors	Trend Indicator	Trend Indicator	Critical
Total Pageviews	Not Important	Not Important	Critical
Average Pageviews per Visit	Trend Indicator	Good	Critical

Relative importance of site metrics based on site type. **Critical** goals should be measured and improved. **Trend** indicators can tell you if your site is headed in the right direction. **Good** means that it's something to keep your eyes on but it's not a primary indicator. Don't waste your time with **Not Important** indicators.

Beyond these, there are certain internal numbers you may want to track, especially for a lead-generation site. For example, you may keep a log of web-leads after they go to the sales department. Wouldn't it be great to know if leads from a certain keyword or web site turn into deals more often than other types of leads? Integrating your web site with a good **CRM (Customer Relationship Management)** suite can show you these types of things. Examples of CRM include SalesForce.com, SugarCRM, and my personal favorite, ZohoCRM, which is free for the first few users.

Critical metrics common to all sites

Regardless of how you do it, most commercial web sites have one very specific goal—increased revenue and profits. So, your metrics should reflect that goal.

- **Total Revenue** (total intake): Revenue, sales, cash or turnover—it's the key driver to a web site's success. You can use Google Analytics to set up revenue goals. For lead generation and ad-driven sites, you'll probably need to continue to track through to your internal reporting infrastructure using something like a CRM or ad-tracking software. Revenue is expressed in dollars: 'We had $50,000 in revenue from our web site in June'.

- **Total Profit** (revenue - expenses): Revenue is top-line; profit is bottom line—what's left over at the end after you fully process each order. This calculation may vary depending on your cost of fulfillment (800#, credit card fees, telephone operator salary, and so on) but it's ultimately why businesses deploy web sites. With lead generation and ad-driven sites, it may take months to have all the data you need to make this calculation, but it's well worth the effort. Total profit is expressed in dollars: 'We had $5,200 in profit from our web site in June'.

Critical e-commerce metrics

The e-commerce web sites have unique critical indicators that set them apart from other types of sites. They tend to be focused on making the sale now, getting the credit card, and shipping the product—the metrics reflect this. Examples of e-commerce web sites include ticket sales, books, CDs, videos, and even **SAAS (software as a service)** web sites. While the SAAS business model isn't exactly e-commerce, the web site certainly can be.

- **Profit per order** (profit / orders): Profit per order is an indicator of the average profit each web site sale generates. Many companies have a steady stream of high volume, low margin products — the **bread and butter** of their business; and a limited number of low-volume, high-margin products that create great **one-off** profitability events. If your site has a mixture of high-margin and low-margin products, it would make sense to measure them separately.

- **Gross profit margin** (sales / cost of the items sold): Depending on your accounting system, you may also need to subtract the cost of sales (which may include ad costs and any commissions paid). Typically, analytics packages aren't robust enough to track this level of detail so you'll need an accounting or reporting system to calculate these numbers for you. Integrating web site analytics into your internal accounting tools is a difficult process that usually requires an outside specialist. But, it can make or break an e-commerce site's profitability. Profit margin is expressed in a percentage: 'The average profit margin of our online sales was 26% in October, which increased to 32% during the Christmas buying season'.

- **Conversions**: The number of sales your site generates is a key metric from which several others can be derived. Ultimately, more sales are a good thing but it's a raw statistic that needs careful scrutiny. Everybody remembers the heady early days at Amazon.com where their sales were increasing by millions of orders per quarter — and they were losing money on every order. It wasn't until they started charging for shipping, and increasing their margin that they started turning huge profits. So, unless you've got money to burn, work to increase your conversions but not at the expense of good profit on each order. Conversions are simple numbers: 'We had 350 sales from our web site in May.'

- **Conversion rate** (number of conversions / the total number of visitors): This metric measures two things: the value of the traffic that is coming to the site and the ability of the site to turn visitors into paying customers. If your conversion rate is low, is it because you're attracting the wrong visitors or is it because your web site isn't credible and easy to use?

- **Average cost per conversion** (cost of advertising / number of transactions): This is similar to profit per order but it measures the cost of acquiring each order. This metric is often used in **pay-per-click** (**PPC**) campaigns. For SEO, it's quite high in the beginning but then steadily drops towards zero. The following screenshot shows average cost per conversion comparison between SEO and PPC:

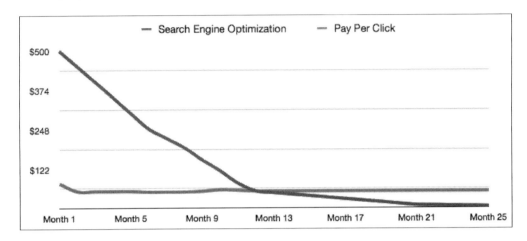

As you can see from this chart, SEO can be very expensive in the beginning but over time (typically in about a year), it beats PPC in cost per conversion. That's because you're not paying for each click with SEO the way you are with Google Adwords and the other Paid Search providers. The high cost in the beginning is an investment in higher rankings. Once you're there, that cost goes away and is replaced by a minimal cost to maintain the high rankings. Many companies combine SEO and PPC to get the best (and worst) of both worlds—quick, short-term results with high ongoing cost of PPC and high initial expense but ultimately low cost per conversion with SEO.

Critical lead generation metrics

Lead generation sites are focused on getting people to contact them. Examples include real estate agents, attorneys, insurance companies, and web design agencies.

- **Profit per order** (total profit / orders): This is just as important for lead generation sites in figuring out the profitability of your SEO campaign. In fact, lead-generation sites typically need a higher profit per order than e-commerce sites to turn a profit because there is a lot more that needs to happen after the lead comes in and before they get the sale. Profit per order is expressed in dollars: 'We averaged $860 in profit per order in September'.

- **Conversions** (inquiries and leads): This is an expression of the number of people who are moving toward doing business with you. It's not as definitive a metric for lead generation sites as it is for e-commerce because sales do not necessarily follow inquiries. However, it is a bellwether of future business. If leads are up then your pipeline is fuller and that means more sales in the coming months. It's expressed in a raw number: "We had 50 phone calls from our web site in March' or "We added 50 new leads to our pipeline from our web site in March'.

- **Conversion rate** (leads / visits) Measures the value of the traffic that's coming to your site. If 1000 people visit and you get 50 leads then you have a 5% conversion rate on your web site. Continue to track those leads through your internal systems and you'll get to a real conversion rate. Say you made ten sales. That means your effective conversion rate is only 1% (10 sales / 1000 visits). Conversion rate is a percentage: 'The recent redesign increased our web site conversion rate from 4% to 5%'.

Web leads are different

Web leads are not like other leads and there should be different processes in place to sell to them. For example, people who find you online may be earlier in the buying cycle than those that are referred by a friend. In this case, you might put a drip campaign in place for your Web leads to keep in touch with them and help move them through the buying cycle.

Critical ad-driven metrics

Ad-driven sites are a breed apart. They want eyeballs—and lots of them. The more people who view their site, the more value it has to an advertiser. Particularly, stats like visitors and pageviews are most important; don't ignore quality of visitors, though. If your advertisers aren't seeing sales then ultimately you're going to have a difficult time generating revenue or you may be forced into receiving a percentage of sales, which is difficult to track. Typical ad-driven sites are content focused—news sites, sports, how-to sites, and gossip are all popular.

- **Number of visitors**: This is the raw number of unique visitors to your web site. It's a great metric to take to advertisers, especially if your visitors tend to be in a particular niche. But, counting the number of visitors that visit your site is like counting the number of people who walk by the front of a retail store. If they don't engage then you don't have a business. Make sure you track additional metrics like Bounce Rate and Page Views to add some gravitas to your visitors metric.

Careful that you don't skew your visitors metric

Visitors are one of the easiest metrics to accidentally make a mess of. Some typical examples are that your employees have your web site set as the start page when they open a new browser window; your HR department posted a job on Craigslist so potential hires are checking you out; or your webmaster is updating the site and reloading again and again. All of these will create spikes in your traffic and skew your numbers. Some of them can be addressed with the Google Analytics module by turning off tracking of registered users or admins, but it's nearly impossible to remove all the skewed numbers. Don't rely on the absolute numbers—look for trends in the number of visitors.

- **Total pageviews**: For ad-driven sites, this is the number. It measures the number of total pages of your site that were viewed. It's a raw number: 'We had 97,000 pageviews last month'. Just like visitors, this metric can be easily misunderstood. A high number of pageviews could be an indicator that your site is popular, or it could mean that it's difficult for visitors to find what they're looking for. It's useful—just be sure you investigate what it means.

- **Average pageviews per visit** (total pageviews / visits): measures how many pages each visitor sees. If you're an ad-driven site, the easiest way to increase your ad revenue is to increase this statistic. If you can increase it from two average pageviews per visit to three average pageviews per visit, with the same amount of traffic you'd then see 50% more ad revenue. 'Since adding links to related content at the bottom of each node with the Acquia Solr Search module, we've seen our average pageviews per visit go from 3 to 4.5'.

Secondary metrics worth tracking

Analytics data is great at showing trends in your site's visitors. These trends may be useful for making certain decisions about your site but they're not necessarily the most important focus of your campaign.

- **Natural versus paid visitors**: Be sure, when using analytics, that you're aware of whether you're viewing your natural or paid visitors. If you're not running pay-per-click advertising campaign then this is a moot point. If you know your conversion rate for paid traffic can be critical for the profitability of your campaign. Pay careful attention in Google Analytics because the default setting is to lump all traffic together into one report.

- **Exit pages**: The last page that someone on your site sees before they leave. If it's not the 'Thank you for ordering' page then you should pay attention. If you're seeing a lot of people leaving on one particular page, chances are good that there is something wrong with it. Take a look. How can you make it better and more attractive? Do people need more options or less? How about an exit survey?

- **Bounce rate**: Bounce rate is the percentage of people that enter your site, view the one page they came in on, and then leave. If you wrote a particularly interesting article, that's getting a lot of links, then it may just be that people are coming to read the article and then leaving. This is especially true for how-to articles like 'How to tie a necktie' or 'How to write a testimonial'. People are there to find out something, and then they leave. Keep them around by offering related content. 'Two more ways to tie a necktie' might get them to stick around and read a bit more — if that's your goal. Bounce rate might also be an indicator that your site is targeting the wrong crowd. Maybe you sell windows but people are searching for Microsoft Windows software. It's important to understand what terms are great and which ones are over-used for you to target.

Hits

Hits are just plain bad. You shouldn't use them because they are greatly misunderstood and can be so misleading. This is one of the easiest numbers to fudge — simply add more graphics to your site's banner and your hits will move up. If you're performance-tuning your server then this might be a good metric but from a marketing standpoint, it just doesn't help. Fortunately, this stat has just about gone the way of the dodo. But, you'll still occasionally run into someone who will insist that hits is a good measure of the site. Run from that person, quickly!

Using analytics data to make SEO decisions

Let's say you sell widgets. The metrics you're measuring for each keyword are Rank in Google, Orders, Revenue, Profit and Profit Per Order.. For the sake of simplicity, we'll say that you only sell one product: the widget.

You may end up with a chart similar to the following table:

Keyword	Rank in Google	Orders	Revenue	Profit	Profit Per Order
widget	4	12	$2,400	$540	$45
easy widget	8	14	$2,800	$630	$45
fast widget	11	3	$600	$135	$45

From the look of things, you should focus your efforts on increasing your ranking for easy widgets! If you're on the bottom of page 1 of Google, imagine how much you could sell if you were at the top.

Let's look deeper and we'll see the power of good analytics.

How would cost per conversion affect profit per order? Cost per conversion includes the amount of time on the phone that you spend with customers helping them make a purchasing decision as well as the cost of the 800# and product returns. Let's take another look with these stats added:

Keyword	Rank in Google	Orders	Revenue	Profit	Cost Per Conversion	Profit Per Order
widget	4	12	$2,400	$540	$8	$37
easy widget	8	14	$2,800	$630	$36	$9
fast widget	11	3	$600	$135	$7	$38

Now, with that single data point, you see that it's probably in your best interest to put your SEO resources into the terms widget and fast widget. With their far lower cost per conversion, these terms are far more profitable per order.

Finding conversion problems with usability testing

Usability testing is an easy and objective way to find out what problems users are going to have with your site. Although it's used widely, some call it the secret weapon of web design because it is so often ignored by site designers. The reasons are many, from arrogance to lack of client support to funds. However, in this day where a 1% increase in web site usability can mean a 50% increase in sales, do not leave this tool in the box.

> "*Debates about the thickness of the drop shadow on the navigation tend to fade in importance as soon as the team sees a prospect struggling to find the Add to Cart button*". - Lance Loveday & Sandra Niehaus, Web Design for ROI

Just a few years ago, usability testing meant renting a $5000 per-day lab with two-way mirrors, and expensive eye-tracking software. With the advent of cheap broadband and web conferencing tools, you can roll your own low-end usability lab for less than $2000. It looks something like the following table:

Item	Purpose	Cost
2 Laptops with built-in camera & microphone (only one is needed if you are just doing remote testing)	For the subject to use during the test and for you to see what the subject is doing	PC: $600 each Mac: $750 each (Check www.eBay.com for better deals.)
Video Chat software (both computers)	To see and hear a video of the subject	Skype (www.skype.com): Free
Web conferencing software (both computers)	So that you can see what the subject is doing on their screen	Cross-platform GoToMeeting (www.gotomeeting.com) makes it easy: $50 per month for unlimited usage. On the Mac you can use iChat which is included free with Mac OS X.
Screen Capture Software (your computer)	To record everything as it comes across your computer.	PC: Camtasia Studio: $299 Mac: iShowU (www.shinywhitebox.com): $29.95
External Hard drive (optional)	If you're going to be doing a lot of usability testing, you're going to need some auxiliary storage to hold all that video	Drobo USB2 or Firewire drive kits (www.drobo.com) are fast, reliable, redundant, and offer almost unlimited expandability. $499 + $200 for a couple of drives.

With these tools, you've got everything you need to do basic usability testing. The high-end labs will offer more, of course, but this solution should provide you with enough insight into the experience visitors are having on your web site. Moreover, since it's there whenever you need it, you'll be far more likely to use it when the time is right.

The design process with usability testing

The macro process should look something like this:

1. Design.
2. Usability test the design, round 1.
3. Adjust design.
4. Usability test the design, round 2.
5. Adjust design.
6. Usability test the design, round 3.
7. Adjust design.
9. Launch site.

Each round of usability testing will reveal issues that you need to improve in your design.

The process for each user

The following is the process that every user follows:

> **How many tests?**
> Best practices call for five to six subjects per round of testing—you could go for eight to ten. However, much more than that and it's time consuming; less than five and you're risking a bad sample size.

On-site testing

On-site testing is great if you have ready access to your target audience, good facilities, and are using a version of the web site that isn't available to the public. It's also great if you want to eliminate technical issues with system setup and broadband speeds.

If you're testing at your location, the process for each test subject will be as follows:

1. Decide what it is that you want to test about the design. Is it the checkout? FAQ? Finding out how much something costs? Tracking an order? Whatever it is, this should be something along the lines that you wish for regular users to be able to accomplish on your site. The list should include five to eight items and might look something like this:

You're a small business owner and you need to fix your widget flange. You search for the term **widget flange** on Google and one of the results brought you to this page. Carry out the following steps:

- ° Find the product that will fix your widget flange.

- ° Pick the color you want and add the widget flange fixer to the cart.

- ° Find the return policy. How long do you have before you can return the widget flange if it doesn't work?_____

- ° Check out the following options:

    i. Use credit card number 1234-5678-9101-1112 with expiration 12/12 and CVV 123

    ii. Use a different shipping and billing address as provided here: (provide some addresses)

    iii. Increase the quantity to 2 items

    iv. Select ground shipping. How much would overnight shipping cost? $_____

    v. Use coupon code 1234 to receive a 10% discount

[Do not put these items in the order that they most logically appear on your site if you want to test the back button.]

- ° Now log out of the site.

- ° Go back to the front page and check the status of your order. Find the expected delivery date.

- ° Send an email to customer service asking them to expedite the shipping.

- ° You are finished. Please let the tester know.

2. Schedule test subjects that match your demographic. Craigslist is a great place to find folks looking to pick up an extra buck. You can offer them anything from free food or free products to cash—$20 to $50 is typically enough depending on the time commitment and travel distance. In a hurry or on a budget? Recruit your friends and family. It's not as valid as a random sample but it's much better than no testing at all. (My wife, a Ph.D. genetics lecturer, is the best usability tester I've ever seen.)

3. Prior to each test, prep the systems. This is where laptops and WiFi come in handy. You can do the prep on both systems in the testing room and then carry the observation computer into the next room before you begin.

    ○ Create the Skype call & test the cameras

    ○ Create the GoToMeeting Conference and test

    ○ Set up the screen recording software on the observer system and test record some video

    ○ On the subject computer, arrange the windows so that you can clearly see everything

    ○ Open the browser to the site you're testing

    ○ Set the screen saver so that the screen is not visible

    ○ Put the systems in two separate rooms so that you're not inadvertently influencing the user

4. Hit record and do a dry run of the objectives to make sure you've got all the information you need (like a credit card number or user login) to accomplish each task. This will also create a **control** video to show what should happen if everything goes right.

5. When the subject arrives, thank them for their help and have them fill out a basic demographic questionnaire (gender, race, income, occupation, years experience using the web, or whatever you feel would be helpful).

6. Sit them down in front of the system you want them to use. Ask them not to touch anything until you ask them to begin.

7. Begin recording.

8. Briefly explain the site that you're testing. Ask them to **think out loud** while they're working. That monologue is very valuable to understand the issues they're having. Explain how you'll be observing everything they're doing but are not available to help.

9. Hand them the list of objectives and leave the room.

10. On the observer computer, be sure everything is recording properly. If it's not, fix it but try not to disturb the test subject.

11. Take good notes, noting the start time and time-stamps of the start of each objective and of interesting things that happen. This saves time when you're reviewing the test later.

12. If the subject gets stuck for awhile on one objective, pop your head into the room and tell them to move on. If objectives are dependant on previous items, tell them which one to do next.

13. When they reach the conclusion of the list, thank them for their participation, give them their payment, and walk them to the door.

14. Stop recording.

15. Reset the systems and repeat with each person.

Patterns will emerge that will convince your team about the changes which need to be made.

Remote testing

Remote testing works just like on-site testing except that the user is in their own home or office. You're back in your office, connected to them via broadband with all your tools and systems in place. It's a bit more complicated to get them set up (they'll need Skype and help connecting to GoToMeeting) but it can be helpful and even cheaper.

Remote testing is desirable if your target audience is not available in your city. Say you're testing users in a particular region or people who have certain need that just isn't necessary in your part of the world (like people who use heating oil when your office is in South Texas). It's also terrific if you want to observe people in their native environments. What distractions are going on around them? What incompatibilities will crop up when you least expect it? Something that works great in a quiet, controlled office may fall apart when a subject's chat window pops open every two seconds.

It's worse than you think

Remember that your usability test subjects are motivated to accomplish the tasks you're asking them to do. You're paying them, remember? So, any issues that you find are probably worse than they appear. Customers that can make their purchases anywhere will leave at the slightest provocation.

Reporting the results

Preparing reports are time-consuming, though, so keep them to a minimum if you can. Because Drupal is so flexible, you may find that just implementing the changes indicated by the usability-testing is all the reporting you need to do. Show them the testing and say something like 'Here are the changes that our usability tests showed would help our site sell more widgets'. Be prepared to back up your findings with the videos, however.

If you do need to provide more data, create short highlight videos based on each objective. This should be relatively easy if you have good time-stamps. Remember, you're not creating a Hollywood movie here, you just want to get the point across.

Usability testing is not for the faint of heart, though! Be prepared for all manner of wailing and moaning from the web design team when you show them these results. Stay calm! The data are on your side. If 80% (or even 50%) of the users had a problem with an element that the designer is in love with then chances are good that it's serious enough to rethink and change.

A/B testing with Google Website Optimizer

A great conversion rate is not a destination—it's a journey. To get the most out of that journey, you need to try different things to increase the usability and conversion rate of your web site. One tool to help you do that testing is Google's Website Optimizer. Google Website Optimizer allows you to test and optimize site content and design by simultaneously deploying two different versions of your web site. It's not as hard as it sounds!

For example, say you wanted to test two different calls to action on your home page. One call to action (we'll call it A) is to download a white paper. The other (we'll call it B) says to call right away. Although you could program Drupal to detect and display different blocks for different sets of users, it would be a difficult task and nearly impossible to track properly in your analytics suite.

Instead, load up the two different sets of HTML as options in Google Website Optimizer. In Drupal, paste in the Optimizer's javascript code. That code will dynamically pick one of the versions of your block from Optimizer to show to each visitor. Then it integrates with Google Analytics so that you can see conversions goals based on which version of the site the visitor was viewing at the time.

Using Google Website Optimizer is not for the faint hearted. It takes quite a bit of initial setup. You can make that setup a bit easier with the Google Website Optimizer module for Drupal. This module speeds up the placing of the blocks of code that you'll need on your testing and conversion pages. This module was written and is maintained by Nick Schoonens—username Schoonzie on `www.Drupal.org`. Half of you buy Nick a beverage and the other half send him some cash. Let's see which one he responds to more. That's a bit of A/B testing. Get it?

Setting up a Google Website Optimizer account

Carry out the following steps in order to set up a Google Website Optimizer account:

1. Go to www.google.com/websiteoptimizer.

2. Log in using your Google account (refer to Chapter 1, *The Tools You'll Need*, if you don't already have a Google account). The following screenshot shows the Google Website Optimizer sign in screen:

3. Select your time zone and click on **Continue**.

4. Click on the **Getting Started** button and agree with the terms of service.

Integrating Google Website Optimizer with Drupal

Carry out the following steps in order to integrate Google Website Optimizer with Drupal:

1. Download the Google Website Optimizer module from `http://drupal.org/project/google_website_optimizer` and install it just like a normal Drupal module. Refer to Chapter 1, *The Tools You'll Need*, for step-by-step module installation instructions.

2. Visit the following link, `http://www.yourDrupalsite.com/admin/settings/google_website_optimizer`, or go to your admin screen and click on **Administer | Site Configuration | Google Website Optimizer**. You'll see the Google Website Optimizer Module admin screen, as shown in the following screenshot:

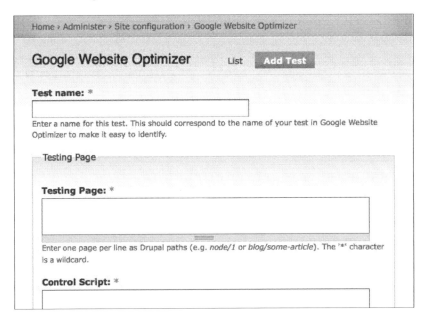

3. Now you need to select or create a testing page and a success page on your site. The testing page is the page where you want to test some variations of your site. The success page is the page that your visitor will see when they have successfully clicked past the testing page. For example, maybe it's a landing page about widgets with a link to the contact us page. The key here is to make sure there is a link from the testing page to the conversions page.

4. Once you have testing and success pages selected or created, decide which element of the page you would like to test. For example, maybe you would like to test the headline of the page.

5. Now, go to the Google Website Optimizer site and click **Create a new experiment**.

6. Click **Multivariate Experiment**. Agree that you've created the required pages and click **Create**.

7. Name your experiment. Enter in the full URLs of the Test page and the Conversion page and click **Continue**.

8. Select **You will install and validate the JavaScript tags** and click **Continue**.

9. You should now see the testing JavaScript code that you will need to run the test, as shown in the following screenshot:

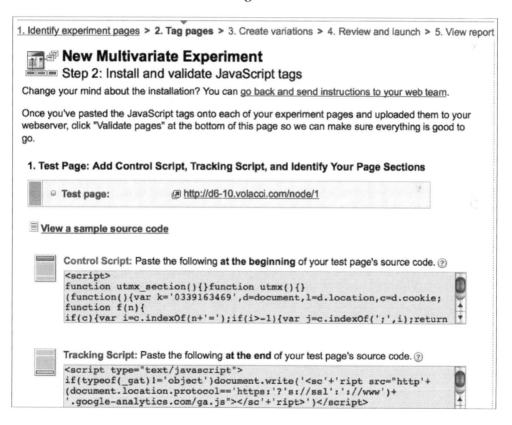

10. Back at the module on your Drupal site, click on **Add test**.

11. Name the test on your Drupal site the same as the test on Google Website Optimizer. This is just for convenience—you could name it anything you want.

12. Under **Testing Page**, enter the Drupal path of the page that you're doing the tests on. Under **Conversion Page**, enter the Drupal path of the page that is your thank you page.

13. Copy and paste the code from Google into the corresponding fields on the module: **Control Script**, **Tracking Script**, and **Conversion Script**.

14. On your Drupal site, click **Create script**. You should see some text confirming **Test created.**

15. Now, you need to tag the sections that you want to test. Navigate to your testing page and put this code immediately before each section you want to test (note that you can copy and paste this code from Google's screen.):

```
<script>utmx_section("Insert your section name here")</script>
```

And paste this text immediately after it:

```
</noscript>
```

Note that in place of `Insert your section name here` text, you need to give a unique name to each testing section.

Drupal does not allow you to insert script code into the node title. If you want to replace the node title of the node (not the title tag, that's different), you'll need to edit your theme files. Find the `page.tpl.php` file for your theme and duplicate it. Rename the new file `page-node-1.tpl.php` and replace the 1 with the number of your testing node. Then, open `page-node-1.tpl.php` and look for this code:

```
<?php if ($title): print '<h2'. ($tabs ? ' class="with-
tabs"' : '') .'>'. $title .'</h2>'; endif; ?>
```

And replace it with this:

```
<?php if ($title): print '<h2'. ($tabs ? ' class="with-
tabs"' : '') .'><script>utmx_section("Insert your
section name here")</script>'. $title .'</noscript></
h2>'; endif; ?>
```

16. Back on Google Website Optimizer, click **Validate pages**. You will see that the Google Website Optimizer JavaScript tags are verified, as shown in the following screenshot:

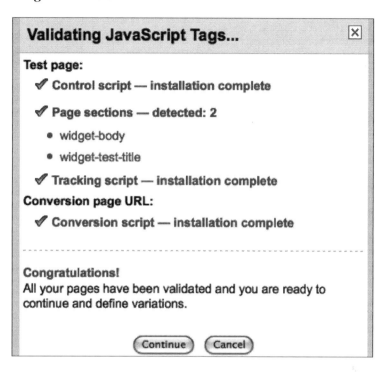

17. Still on Google Website Optimizer, click **Continue** and then click **Continue** again.

18. Now you will create the variations of your content that you will be testing. Click the **Add new variation** link. Name the new variation. Replace the default text with your variation code and click on **Save**.

19. Keep doing this until you have all the variations you want to test. Until you're familiar with this tool, you may want to only use a couple of variations on a single element. When you're done, click **Save and Continue**.

20. Now, click on **Preview this experiment now**. A separate window will open where you should see a page similar to the following screenshot:

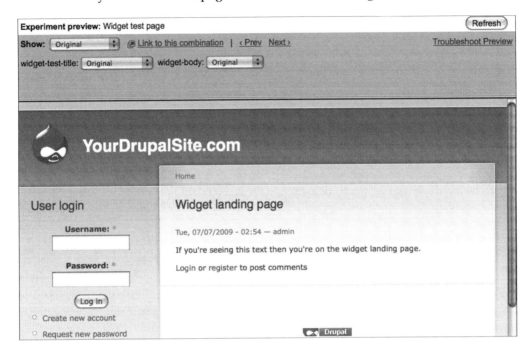

21. You can now select the different variations of your experiment. As you select each combination, you should see the variations that you've set up. Try out all the different combinations to make sure that none of your code combinations break your layout.

22. When you're finished testing, close the testing window and click the **Launch now** button.

23. Your experiment is now running and you have a couple more options:

    ° Total traffic sent through this experiment: It lets you decide if you want all the traffic that visits your testing page to use the testing code. Usually I'll set this to 100% for elements that I haven't tested before. But, if I have a pretty good conversion rate (2 to 3%) then I'll only run half the traffic through it. It takes longer but I'm not risking losing many conversions by running the test.

    ° Auto-disable losing variations will turn off combinations that are performing poorly allowing you a true 'set it and forget it' experiment. There are three options: Conservative, Moderate, and Aggressive. Conservative will only turn off the variation when it's getting way less conversions than the original. Moderate will turn off the variation when it's significantly lower. Aggressive will turn it off even when it's just a little lower. For most experiments, I like the Moderate setting.

24. You should begin to see statistics within three hours.

The more traffic you have, the quicker you can test out the different options. Depending on the traffic to the testing page, you may be able to start making conversion decisions in a few hours. But, don't worry if it takes you several days or weeks of testing to see an obvious pattern. I like to allow at least 100 visitors to see each variation before I make a decision. More if the site is high traffic.

Don't overlook another great feature of the module—A/B testing. A/B testing is similar except that it allows you to test completely different versions of a Drupal page. Imagine that users click on the contact us link and half see a long form and the other half a short form. Which gets more visitors to fill it out? Don't guess, run the experiment.

Regardless of how many tests you run, utilizing multivariate and A/B testing on your site can help you improve your conversion rate on an ongoing basis. Stop guessing, and start testing your design elements. The stats don't lie—you just have to start collecting them.

Summary

No amount of traffic will help your business unless someone is buying your products. A conversion is the science of getting site visitors to do what you want them to do which ultimately means more money for your business.

In this chapter, we have covered the following topics:

- The three different types of web sites: e-commerce, lead-generation, and advertising driven
- Paths to conversions
- Creating strong calls to action
- Analytics to watch based on the type of web site you're working with
- Using analytics to make SEO decisions
- Usability testing
- Multivariate testing with Google Website Optimizer

Implement these techniques and your site will be well on its way to a high conversion rate. Remember, improving your conversion rate is not a destination—it's a journey!

A
10 SEO Mistakes to Avoid

There are several common mistakes that you should avoid when launching an SEO campaign. These are some of them.

1. Not tracking or not tracking the right statistics

Occurs when

You don't have any Analytics software installed.

Fix by

It can be fixed by installing Analytics as soon as you launch the site. Refer to Chapter 1, *The Tools You'll Need*.

2. Picking keywords that don't produce enough traffic

Occurs when

You pick terms that match your product or service but don't check to make sure that your customers actually use those terms. Great rankings don't mean a thing if nobody searches for those terms.

Fix by

It can be fixed by picking terms that are targeted but also produce some good traffic. It will take you longer to rank but you'll get a lot more out of it when you finally do. Refer to Chapter 2, *Keyword Research*.

3. Duplicating content

Occurs when

You have the exact same content on two or more pages on your site. Drupal does this when clean URLs are turned on.

Fix by

It can be fixed by installing and configuring the Global Redirect Module. Refer to Chapter 3, *On-Page Optimization*.

4. Changing the node path without creating a redirect

Occurs when

You edit a node and change the path. The node is still displaying properly but the old path shows a file not found error.

Fix by

It can be fixed by properly installing and configuring the Path Redirect module. Refer to Chapter 3, *On-Page Optimization*.

5. Spending time on meta tags that don't matter

Occurs when

You go through your site setting keyword and other meta tags on each node.

Fix by

It can be fixed by remembering that Google doesn't use the keywords meta tag. Go ahead and set them for your main pages but don't spend too much time on it.

6. A slow Drupal site

Occurs when

Your site takes more than about two seconds to load.

Fix by

It can be fixed by turning on caching, upgrading your server or changing your hosting company. There are also more advanced caching mechanisms you can use. Refer to Chapter 7, *RSS Feeds, Site Speed, and SEO Testing*.

7. Flash, frames, graphics, and other things are obscuring your site from Google

Occurs when

The site was built more for looks than for ranking well in the search engines.

Fix by

It can be fixed by making sure that your keywords appear in your site—especially on the pages that contain a lot of graphics or Flash.

8. Optimizing for your company name

Occurs when

The company name appears first in the title tags and other places on the site. It's easy to forget that your corporate site will probably rank first in Google for your company name and brand names so there's probably no need to optimize for it.

Fix by

It can be fixed by using keywords at the beginning of your title tags and moving your company name to the end. For example: 'Mortgages by Big Bank Corp' instead of 'Big Bank Corp Mortgages'. See Chapter 3, *On-page Optimization*

9. Not putting contact information on the site

Occurs when

Your company phone number or other contact information doesn't appear in the banner of your site which would make it very easy for people to contact you.

Fix by

It can be fixed by putting the phone number big and bold in the banner. Make sure you put it in the footer and other obvious places like the contact us page. Refer to Chapter 10, *Increasing the Conversion Rate of Your Drupal Web site*.

10. Not enough links

Occurs when

There is a belief that if you just put up a good site with good content then you'll rank at the top of Google and the other search engines. While these things help a lot, most sites will need to generate at least a few good links in order to rank.

Fix by

It can be fixed by spending a few hours getting some links. If you're not sure how to do this, it may be worth it to call in an SEO consultant to help you out.

B

A Drupal SEO Checklist

Here's a checklist that you can follow for each Drupal site that you want to optimize. Put things like logins and URLs in the Notes column. Look for updates to this list at the following web site: http://www.DrupalSEObook.com/.

Setup

Task	Date Completed	Notes
Drupal SEO Checklist module		
Create a Google Account		
Create a Google Analytics Account		
Google Analytics module		
Create Google Webmaster Tools Account and verify site		
Set a preferred domain and crawl rate in Google Webmaster Tools		
Install CrazyEgg (optional)		
Install Mint (optional)		
Install Google Toolbar browser plugin		
Install SEO for Firefox browser plugin		

Step 1: Keyword Research

Task	Date Completed	Notes
Set keyword goals		
Top searches module		
Pick keywords		

Keyword list:

Step 2: On Page SEO

Task	Date Completed	Notes
Page title module		
Write page titles		
Turn on Clean URLs		
Path module		
Write optimized URL paths		
PathAuto module		
Path Redirect module		
Global Redirect module		
Adjust H1, H2, H3 in your theme		
Rewrite site navigation using keywords		
Meta tags module		
Set meta tags for nodes or views		
Consider the SEO Compliance Checker module		

Step 3: Technical SEO

Task	Date Completed	Notes
XML Sitemap module		
Submit XML sitemap to Google		
Google News Sitemap module (optional)		
Submit News Sitemap to Google News		
URL List module		
Site Map module		
Fix the Drupal robots.txt file		
Add the XML Sitemap to robots.txt		
Test robots.txt using Google Webmaster Tools		
Adjust your .htaccess file		
Validate using W3C tools		
Syndication module		
Add RSS feeds to site		
Speed up Drupal		
Grade site using SEOmoz tool		

Step 4: Content

Task	Date Completed	Notes
Write great content		
Put keywords in the content		
Test the density		
Optimize category pages		
Setup Google News alerts for ideas		
Build relationships		
Scheduler module		
Build hierarchy into site		
Consider OpenCalais		
Create More Like This blocks		
HTML Purifier module		
Create Mollom account		
Mollom module		
Notify module		

Step 5: Conversions

Task	Date Completed	Notes
Set Conversion goals		
Create Calls to Action		
Set up Analytics to track goals		
Use Analytics data to improve site		
Create paths to conversion diagram		
Track conversions at each point		
Conduct Usability testing		
Create Google Optimizer account		
Google Optimizer module		

C

Drupal SEO Case Study for Acquia Product Launch

About Acquia

Acquia is a Boston-based company that provides commercial support for the open source social publishing system Drupal. Drupal is both a CMS and a social software platform that enables users to publish and manage all types of editorial and user-generated content on the web—for example, a corporate web site, a social networking site, or a multi-user blog. As a commercial vendor for Drupal, Acquia helps organizations large and small meet their web-related business goals using Drupal based web sites.

Problem

In March of 2008, Acquia launched their company and web site in preparation for their eventual product release. This start-up company faced the challenge of entering an already crowded field, and was virtually invisible to the communities they were trying to reach on the web. They recognized that **Search Engine Optimization (SEO)** was essential from the get-go.

Solution

Acquia's goal is to be a trusted source of information and support for Drupal. Enter Volacci, an internet marketing firm that specializes in natural SEO. Volacci partnered with Acquia in May of 2008 to provide content optimization, conversions consulting, and link-building solutions for www.Acquia.com.

To optimize their site's content, Volacci advised Acquia on the implementation of specific Drupal modules for SEO. These modules included Pathauto, XML Sitemap, and others. Then, the site's content, HTML, and structure were modified to better communicate to the search engines that Acquia is an authority on Drupal. Consequently, its attractiveness to both visitors and search engines was enhanced.

Volacci also provided recommendations to maximize the conversion rate. Increasing the rate at which visitors to the web site download or purchase Acquia subscriptions directly affects the bottom line, so this was an important consideration. Volacci worked with the Acquia team to identify high-quality content and improve its utilization on the site to maximize conversions.

Results

Volacci provides its clients with detailed tracking reports on a weekly basis to measure progress. When Acquia was ready to launch their product in September, they had achieved a significant increase in market awareness with the help of a drastic increase in their Google ranking. If we look at the search ranking of two highly-competitive terms over the first six months of the campaign, the results are striking:

Google ranking

The following screenshot shows the highest rank achieved in Google as of October 31, 2008:

Term Searched	May	October
"drupal"	65	5
"content management system"	not listed	11

Clearly, the combination of high quality, targeted content and SEO in partnership with Volacci has propelled Acquia to the top of the search engines. Comparing the first thirty days with Volacci (May, 2008) to the sixth month (October, 2008):

- Site visits from search engines increased by an incredible 270%

- The bounce rate decreased by 8% (from 48% down to 40%)

- Average time spent on the web site doubled (from 7.5 to 15 minutes), with the number of pages per visit up by 35% (from 3.2 to 4.3)

"SEO was a key part of making the launch successful and contributing to the organic search traffic gains at a crucial time in our evolution — when market visibility was critical" - Bryan House, Director of Marketing at Acquia

Visitors to Acquia.com

It's clear from examining both the Google ranking and traffic to the web site that Volacci's team met the challenge. Volacci helped Acquia maximize its web visibility, leading to a dramatic increase in the quantity and quality of web traffic, setting the stage for a successful product launch.

Index

C

Calais. *See* **Open Calais**
case study
  Acquia Product Launch 249
CCK
  URL 94
CCK ninja 94
clean URLs
  about 68
  turning on 68
comment
  spam, preventing 204
comment, robots.txt command 134
comments, monitoring
  about 209
  Mollom, feedback providing to 209, 210
  Notify module used 209
competitors website for keywords,
      scrapping
  easy way 45
  quick way 45
content
  about 167, 168
  attention, grabbing 168
  body 169
  bulk processing, Open Calais used 195, 196
  catchy headline 168
  forms 167
  Google News Alerts, setting up 174, 175
  headlines, example 169
  HTML Purifier module 201
  keywords, selecting 169
  linking, to others 180
  newsreaders 176-179
  organizing, Drupal used 184
  relationship, building 180
  removing 186, 187
  Scheduler module, downloading 182-184
  search engine optimizing 171
  writing 168, 179
  writing, for audience 173
  writing, inspiration 181, 182
content, body
  Base Site Pages 170
  supplemental pages 170, 171

Content Construction Kit. *See* **CCK**
content, organizing
  about 185
  Drupal used 184
  keywords, building into categories 185
  site, structuring 184
  structured URL paths, creating 186
  taxonomy used 186
content path
  changing 70, 71
Content Refresh Module 163
conversion
  ad-driven path, process 215
  Ad-driven site, goal 212
  Add to Cart button 216
  considerations 212
  Contact Us link 216
  e-commerce path, process 214
  e-commerce site, goal 212
  enhancing, ways 216
  freebies, for customers 217
  goals 212
  issues finding, usability testing used 224,
      225
  lead generation paths, process 214
  lead generation site, goal 212
  path to 213
  phone number 216
  strong calls, incorporating 216
conversions, keyword goals
  lead generation 42
  page impression (or ad impression) 42
  transaction 41
  types 41
crawl delay, robots.txt command 134
crawler 30
CrazyEgg 32
credibility, keyword goals
  product brand awareness 41
CRM 218
Cron 116
Custom JavaScript Code field 25
Customer Relationship Management. *See*
      CRM

Google News XML Sitemap
  generator module, setting up 121
  submitting, to Google news 123
Google's Webmaster Tools
  Analyze robots.txt 142, 143
  Googlebot 145
  Googlebot-Image 144, 145
  using, to evaluate robots.txt file 141-145
Google Toolbar
  about 33
  PageRank 33
Google Trends 48
Google Webmaster Tools
  about 25
  crawl rate 29
  crawl rate, setting 29, 30
  preferred domain, setting 29
  settings 28
  site, verifying 26-28
Google Website Optimizer
  about 17, 230
  integrating, with Drupal 232-237
  setting up, steps 231
Google Zeitgeist 47

H

H1 88
hanging heading tag
  avoiding 88
headings
  about 87
  handling 89
  hanging heading tag, avoiding 88
  HTML header tags 88
heading tags
  front page, of site 89
  lists 89
  single node view 89
HTML Purifier 14
HTML Purifier module
  downloading 201-203

I

ImageField module
  URL 94
ImageField tokens
  URL 94
images
  optimizing 92
internal feed alias text, Pathauto
  Taxonomy term path, settings 77
  user path, settings 77

J

JavaScript tags, validating 235

K

key phrases 38
keyword
  about 38
  aggregate searchers, into organized groups
    38
  goals 40
  market, defining 38, 39
  research, importance 39, 40
keyword density 172
Keyword Discovery 49
keyword, goals
  brand awareness 40
  company brand awareness 40
  conversions 41
  conversions, types 41
  credibility 41
  lead generation 41
  page impression (or ad impression) 42
  product brand awareness 40
keyword research
  importance 39, 40
keyword research, tools
  competitors website for keywords,
    scrapping 45
  Google Adwords Keyword Tool 46
  Google Trends 48

[PACKT] PUBLISHING

Thank you for buying
Drupal 6 Search Engine Optimization

Packt Open Source Project Royalties

When we sell a book written on an Open Source project, we pay a royalty directly to that project. Therefore by purchasing Drupal 6 Search Engine Optimization, Packt will have given some of the money received to the Drupal project.

In the long term, we see ourselves and you—customers and readers of our books—as part of the Open Source ecosystem, providing sustainable revenue for the projects we publish on. Our aim at Packt is to establish publishing royalties as an essential part of the service and support a business model that sustains Open Source.

If you're working with an Open Source project that you would like us to publish on, and subsequently pay royalties to, please get in touch with us.

Writing for Packt

We welcome all inquiries from people who are interested in authoring. Book proposals should be sent to author@packtpub.com. If your book idea is still at an early stage and you would like to discuss it first before writing a formal book proposal, contact us; one of our commissioning editors will get in touch with you.

We're not just looking for published authors; if you have strong technical skills but no writing experience, our experienced editors can help you develop a writing career, or simply get some additional reward for your expertise.

About Packt Publishing

Packt, pronounced 'packed', published its first book "Mastering phpMyAdmin for Effective MySQL Management" in April 2004 and subsequently continued to specialize in publishing highly focused books on specific technologies and solutions.

Our books and publications share the experiences of your fellow IT professionals in adapting and customizing today's systems, applications, and frameworks. Our solution-based books give you the knowledge and power to customize the software and technologies you're using to get the job done. Packt books are more specific and less general than the IT books you have seen in the past. Our unique business model allows us to bring you more focused information, giving you more of what you need to know, and less of what you don't.

Packt is a modern, yet unique publishing company, which focuses on producing quality, cutting-edge books for communities of developers, administrators, and newbies alike. For more information, please visit our website: www.PacktPub.com.

Drupal 6 Content Administration

ISBN: 978-1-847198-56-3   Paperback: 196 pages

Maintain, add to, and edit content of your Drupal site with ease

1. Keep your Drupal site up to date: easily edit, add to, and maintain your site's content, even if you've never used Drupal before!

2. Covers the full range of content that you might want on your site: richly formatted text, images, videos, as well as blog posts, calendar events, and more

3. Get to grips with managing users, slaying spam, and other activities that will help you maintain a content-rich site

Drupal for Education and E-Learning

ISBN: 978-1-847195-02-9   Paperback: 400 pages

Teaching and learning in the classroom using the Drupal CMS

1. Use Drupal in the classroom to enhance teaching and engage students with a range of learning activities

2. Create blogs, online discussions, groups, and a community website using Drupal.

3. Clear step-by-step instructions throughout the book

4. No need for code! A teacher-friendly, comprehensive guide

Please check **www.PacktPub.com** for information on our titles

4064048

Made in the USA
Lexington, KY
17 December 2009